FAR FROM THE MADDING COW!

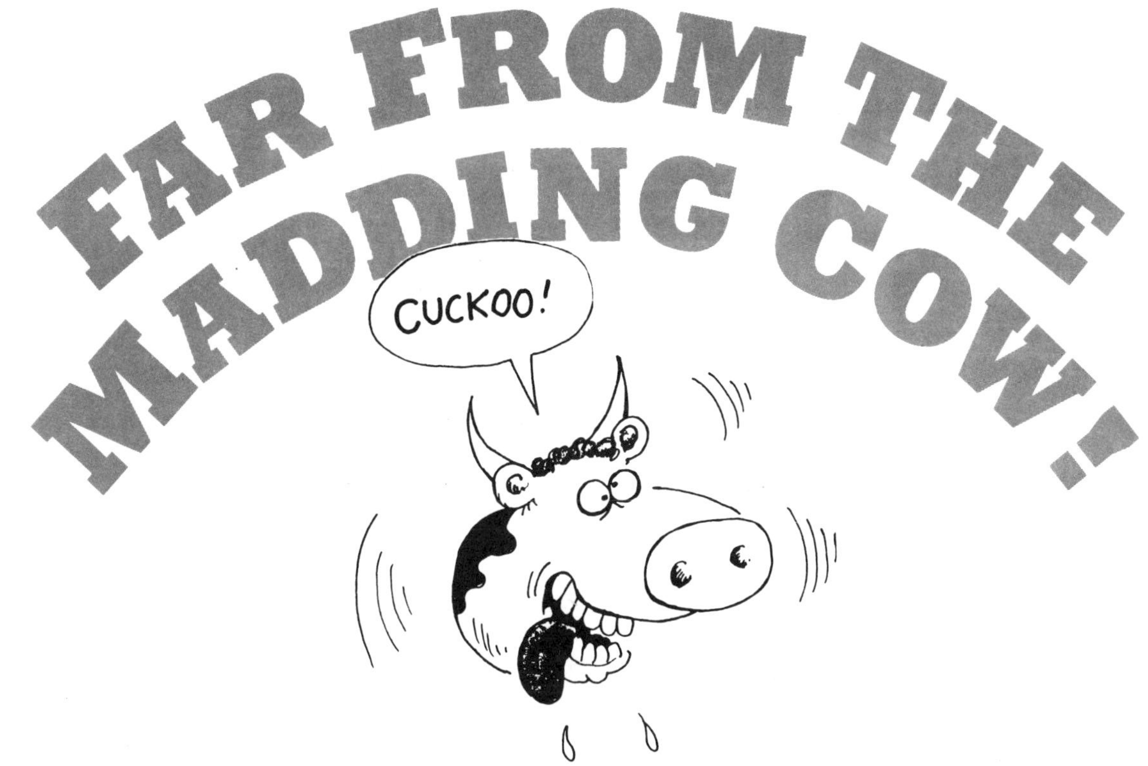
CUCKOO!

CARTOONS BY

DAVID AUSTIN, NICK NEWMAN and KIPPER WILLIAMS

MAINSTREAM PUBLISHING

Copyright © David Austin, Nick Newman and Kipper Williams, 1990

First published in Great Britain in 1990 by
MAINSTREAM PUBLISHING COMPANY (EDINBURGH) LTD
7 Albany Street
Edinburgh EH1 3UG

British Library Cataloguing in Publication Data

Austin, David *1935-*
Far from the madding cow.
1. English humorous cartoons collections
I. Title II. Newman, Nick   III. Williams, Kipper *1951-*
741.5942

ISBN 1-85158-323-8

Printed in Great Britain by Scotprint Ltd., Musselburgh

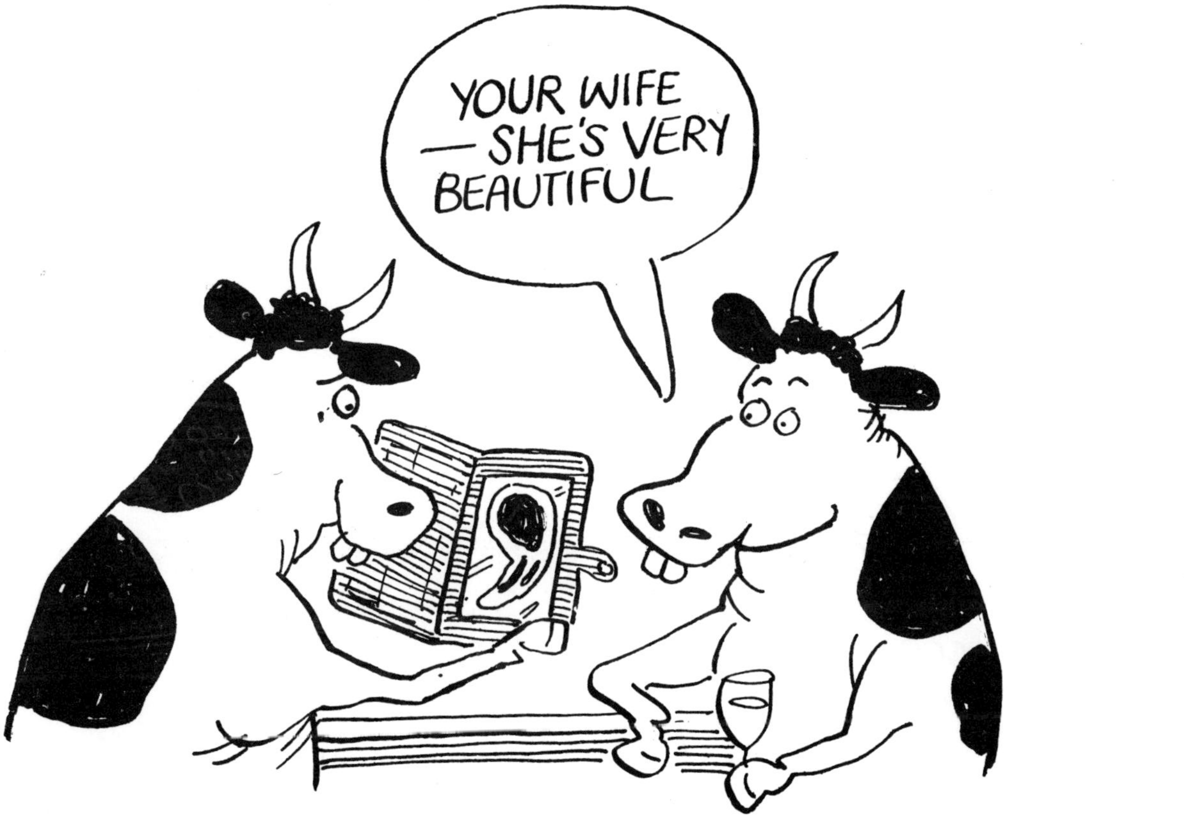
YOUR WIFE — SHE'S VERY BEAUTIFUL

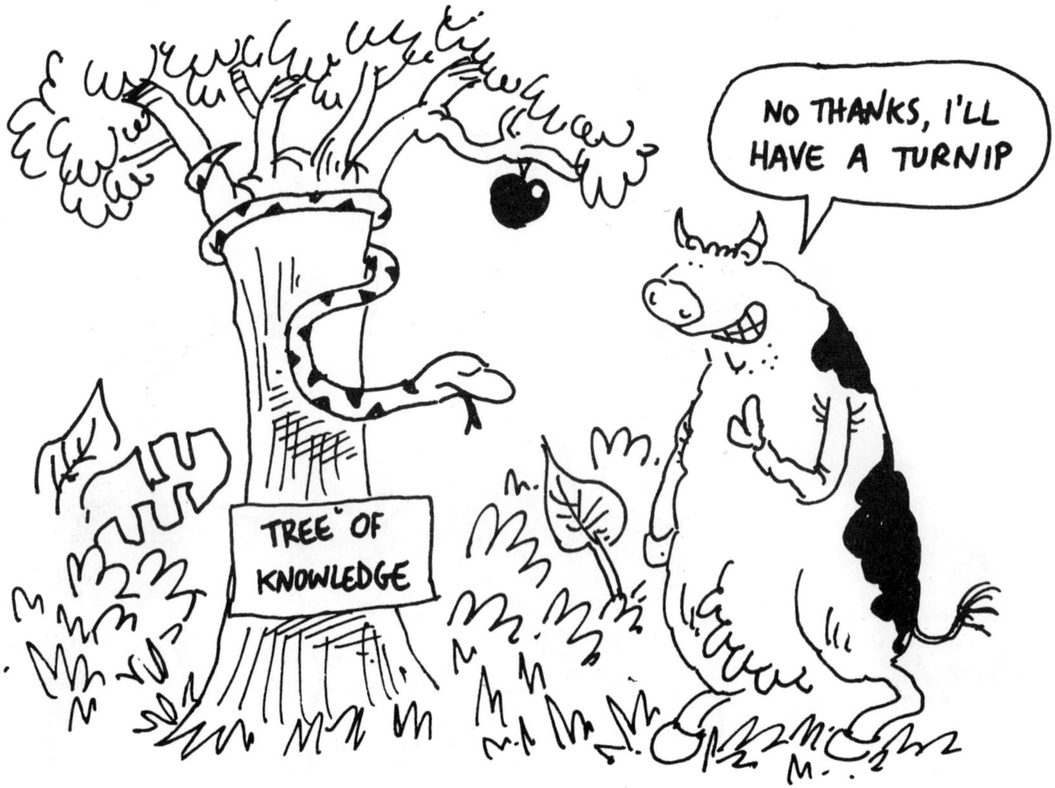
NO THANKS, I'LL HAVE A TURNIP
TREE OF KNOWLEDGE

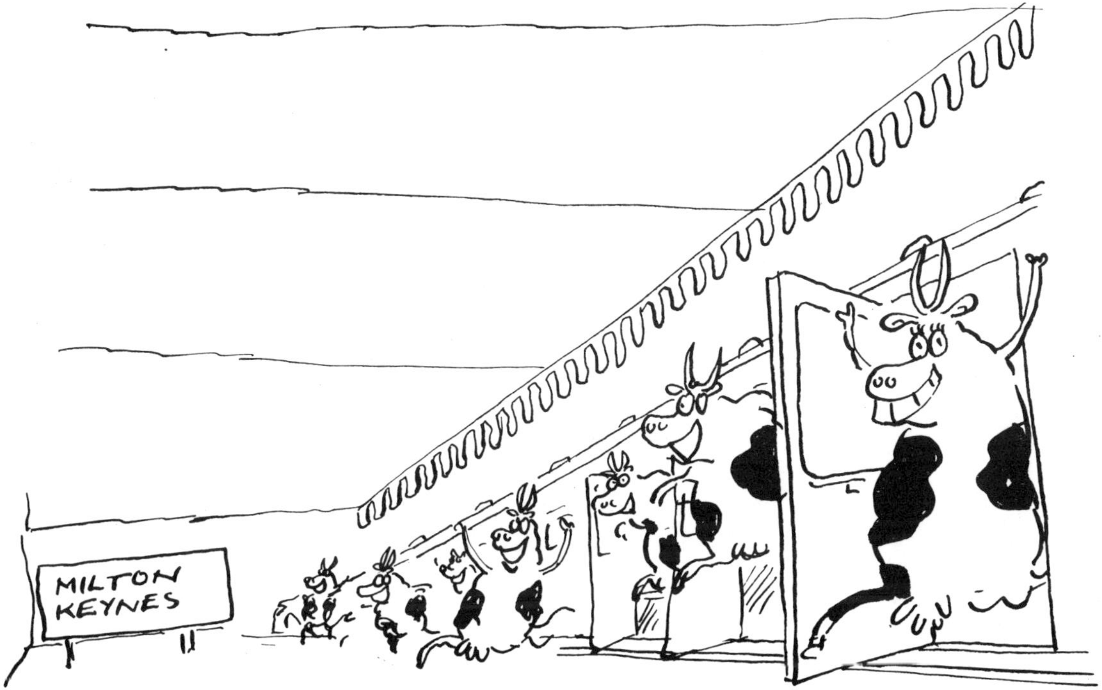
MILTON
KEYNES

SELLAFIELD
VISITORS'
CENTRE
LUNCH

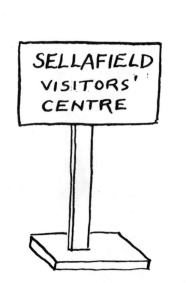

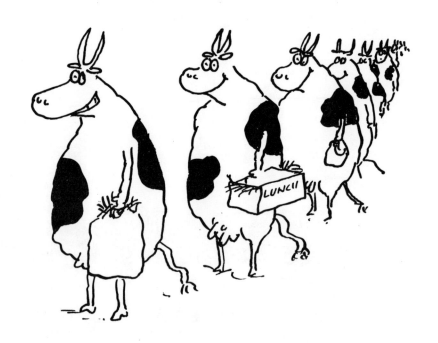

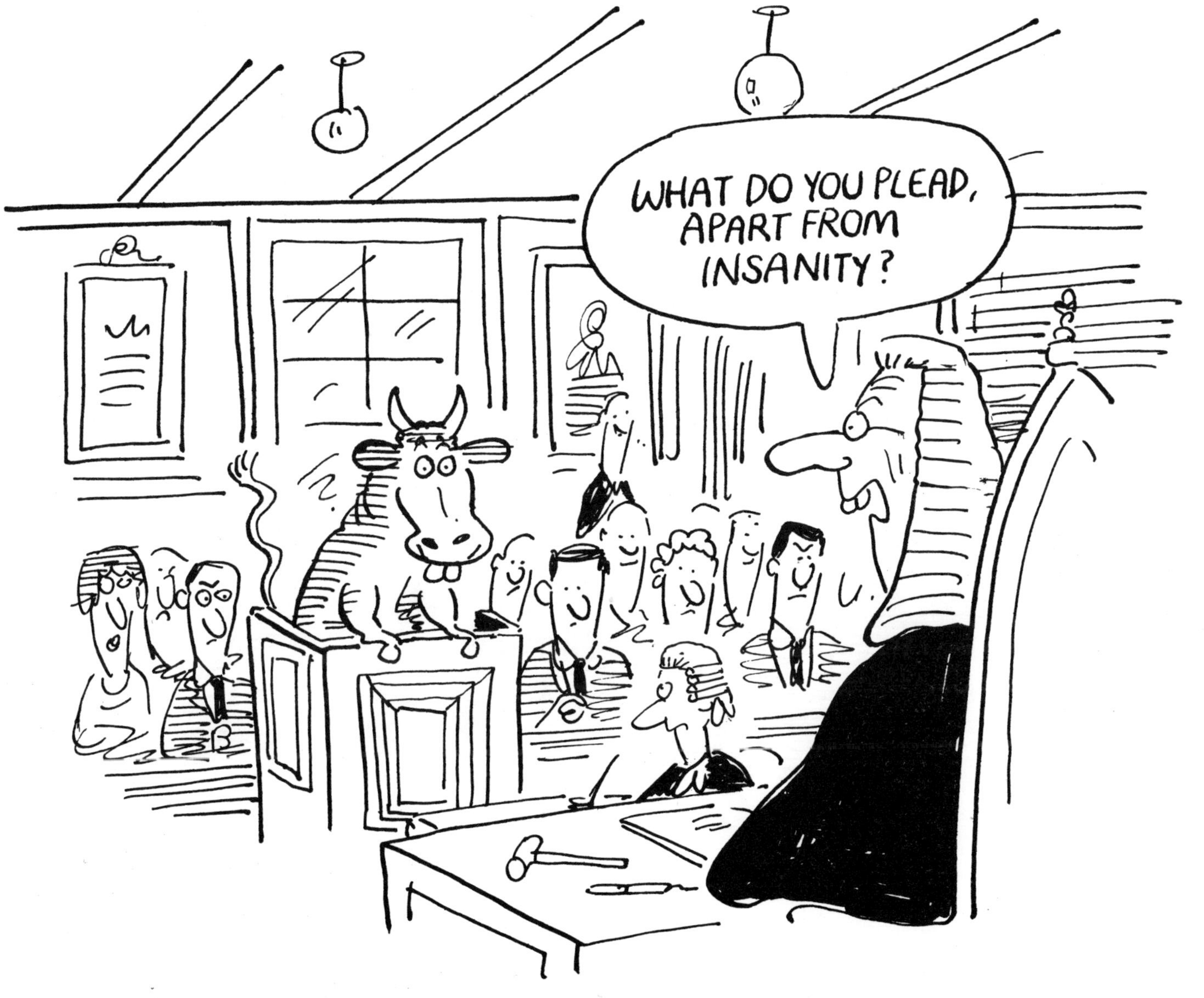
WHAT DO YOU PLEAD, APART FROM INSANITY?

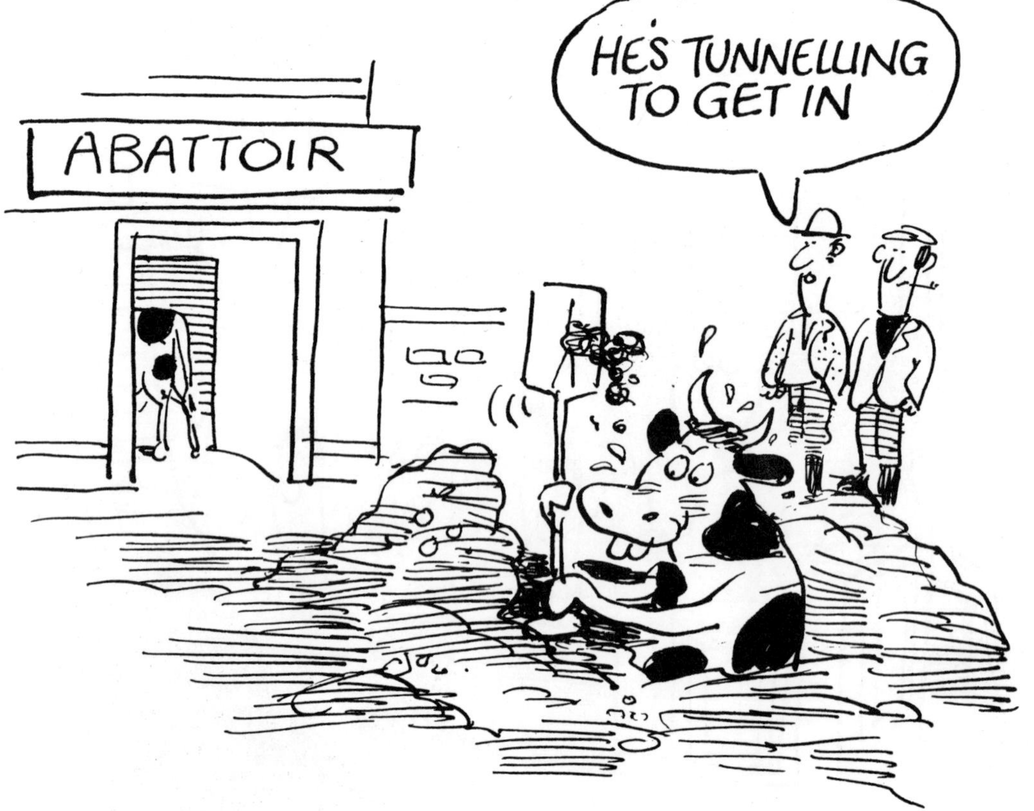
ABATTOIR
HE'S TUNNELLING TO GET IN

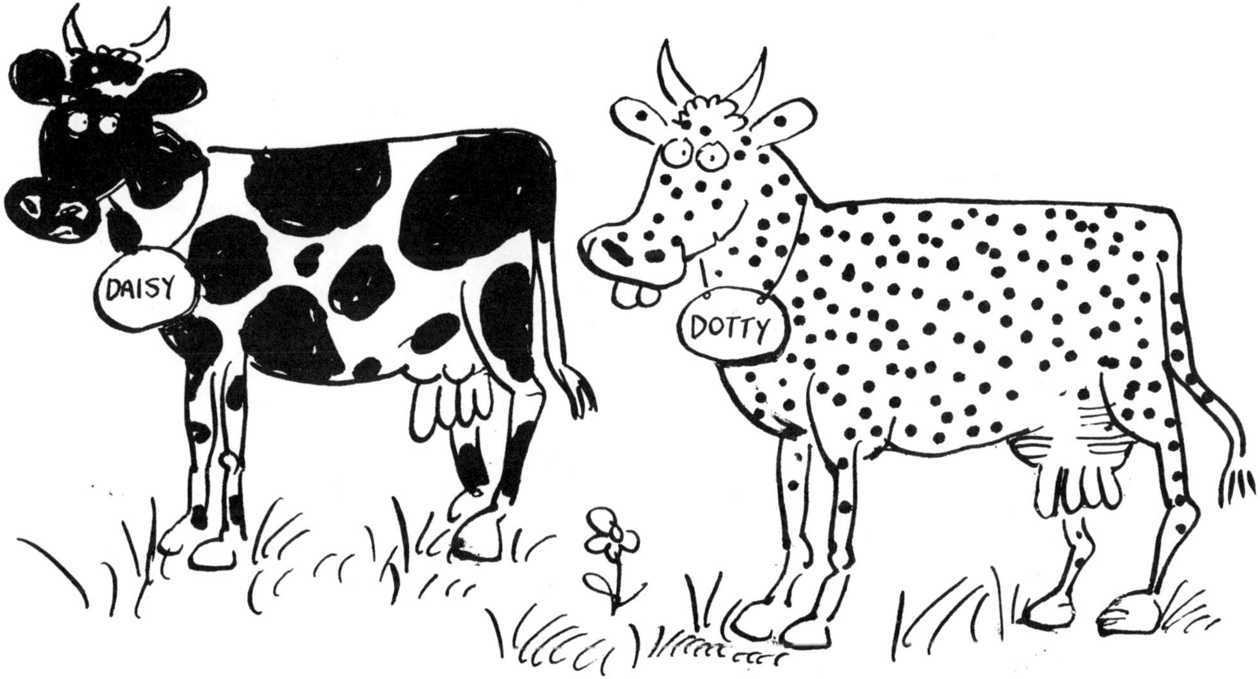
DAISY
DOTTY

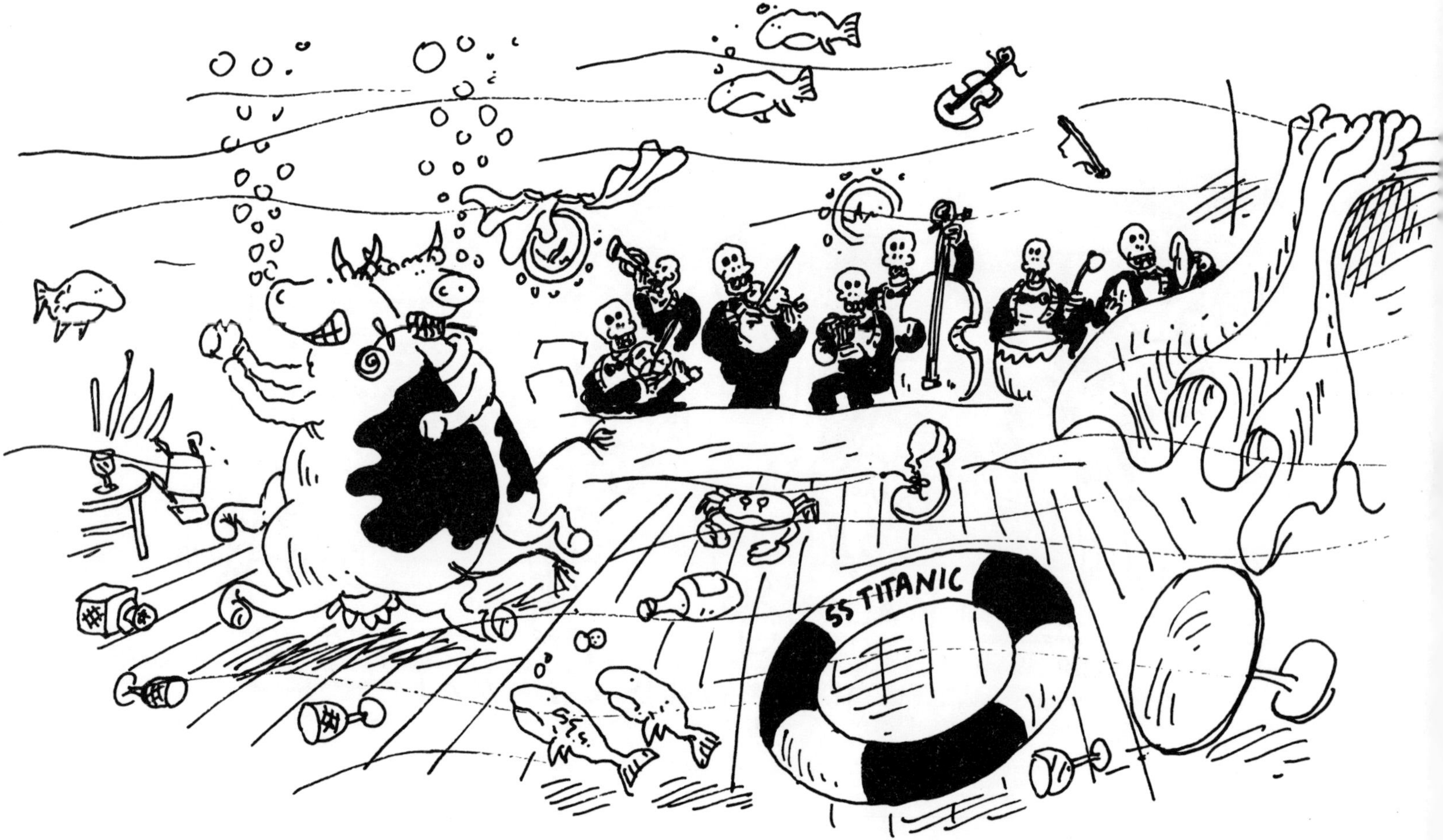
SS TITANIC

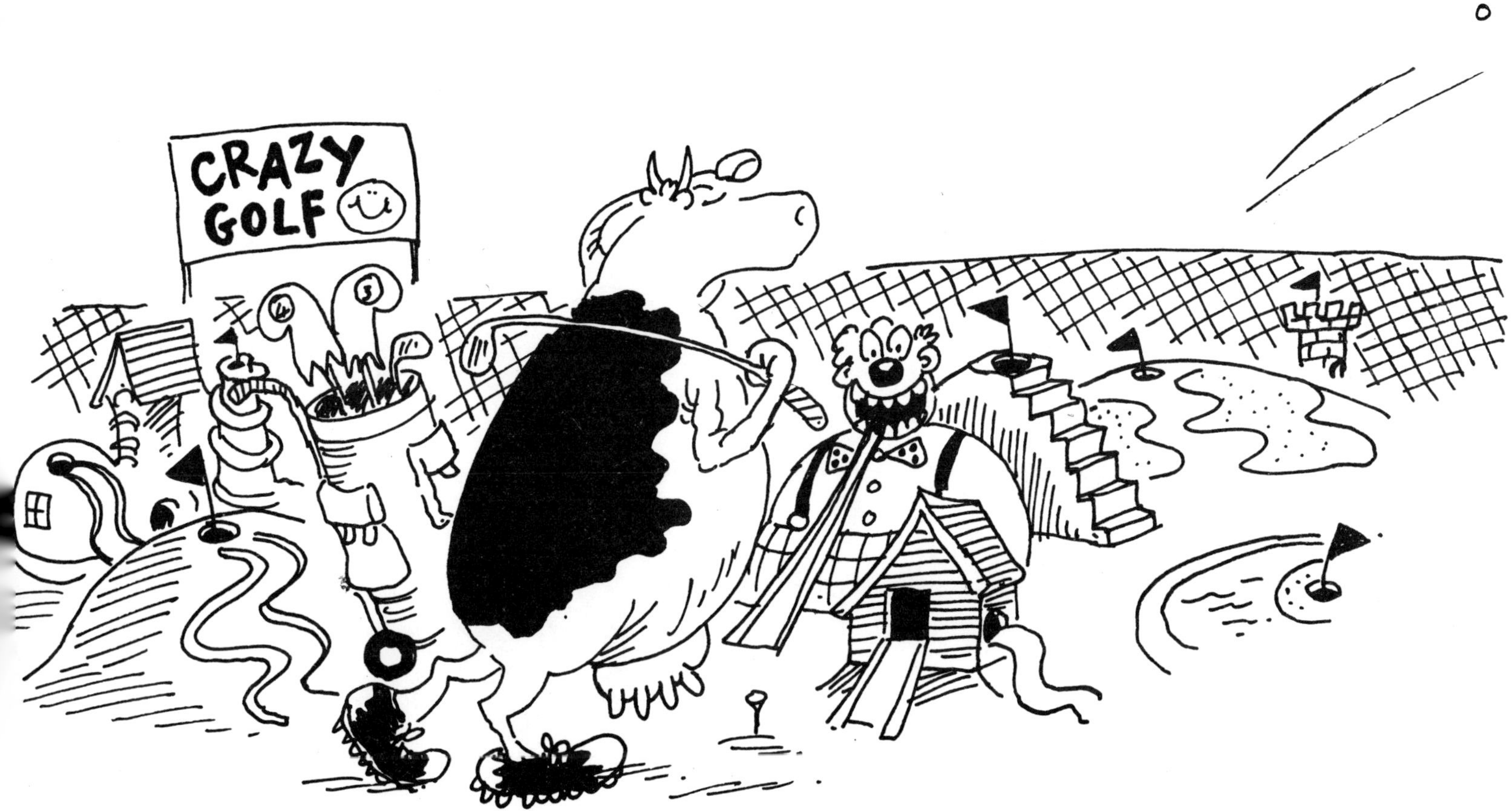
CRAZY
GOLF

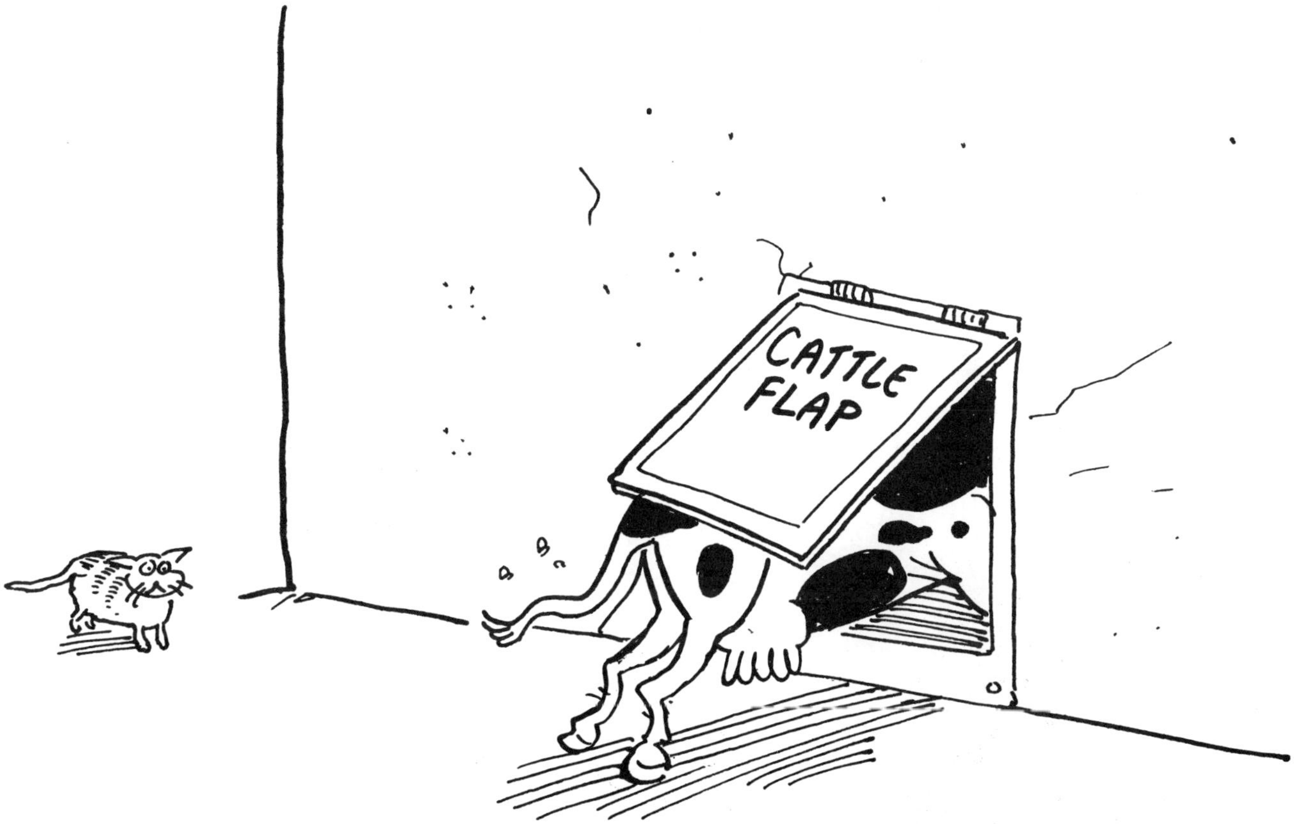
CATTLE FLAP

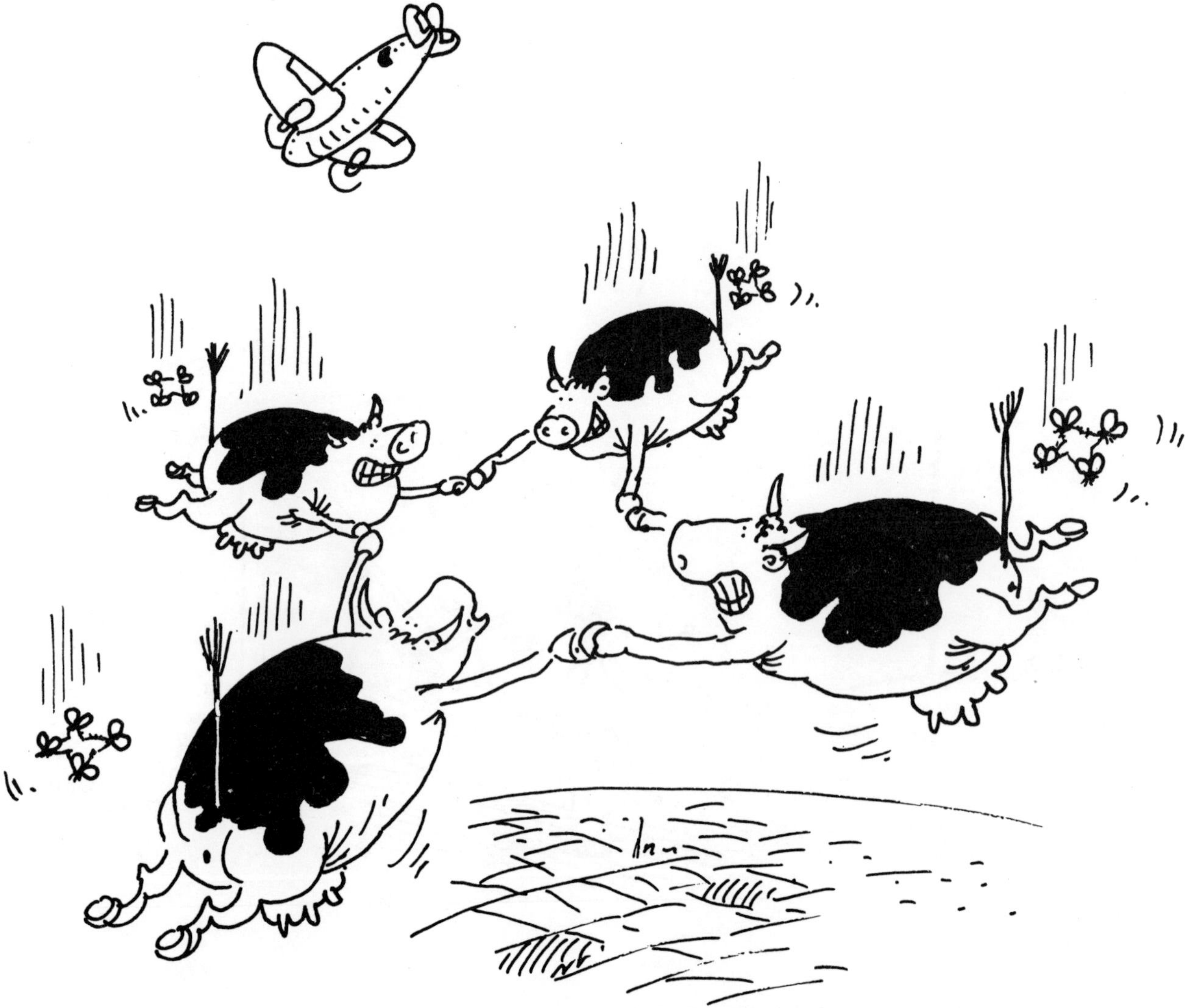

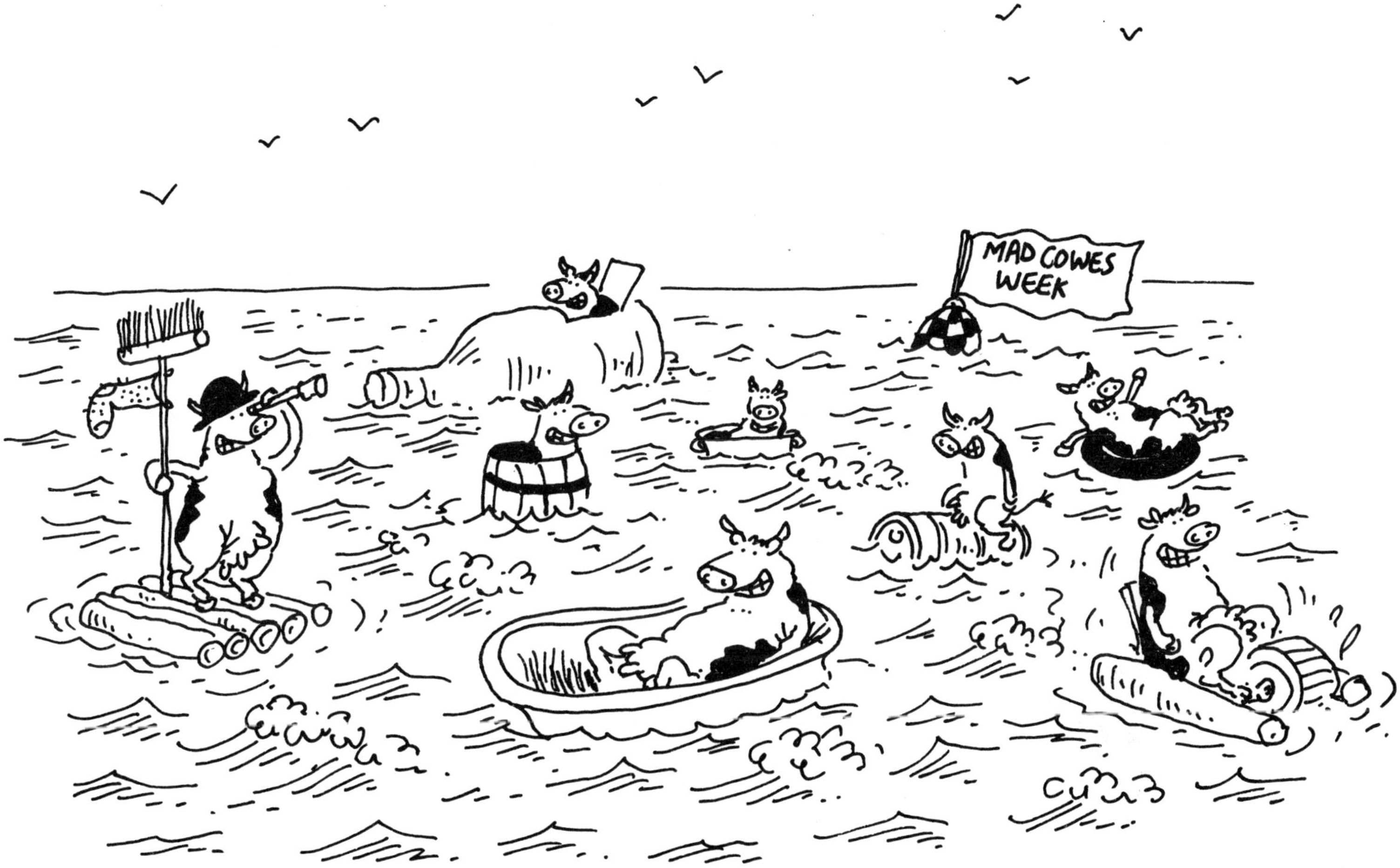
MAD COWES
WEEK

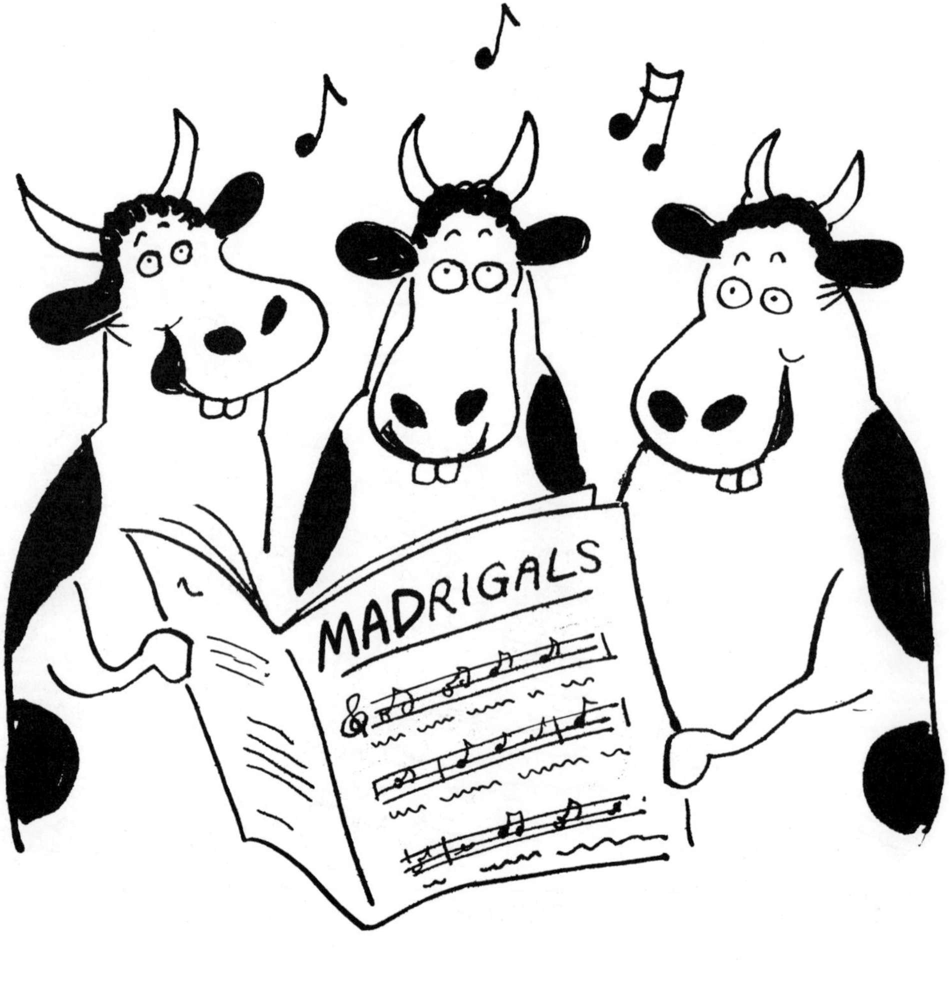
MADRIGALS

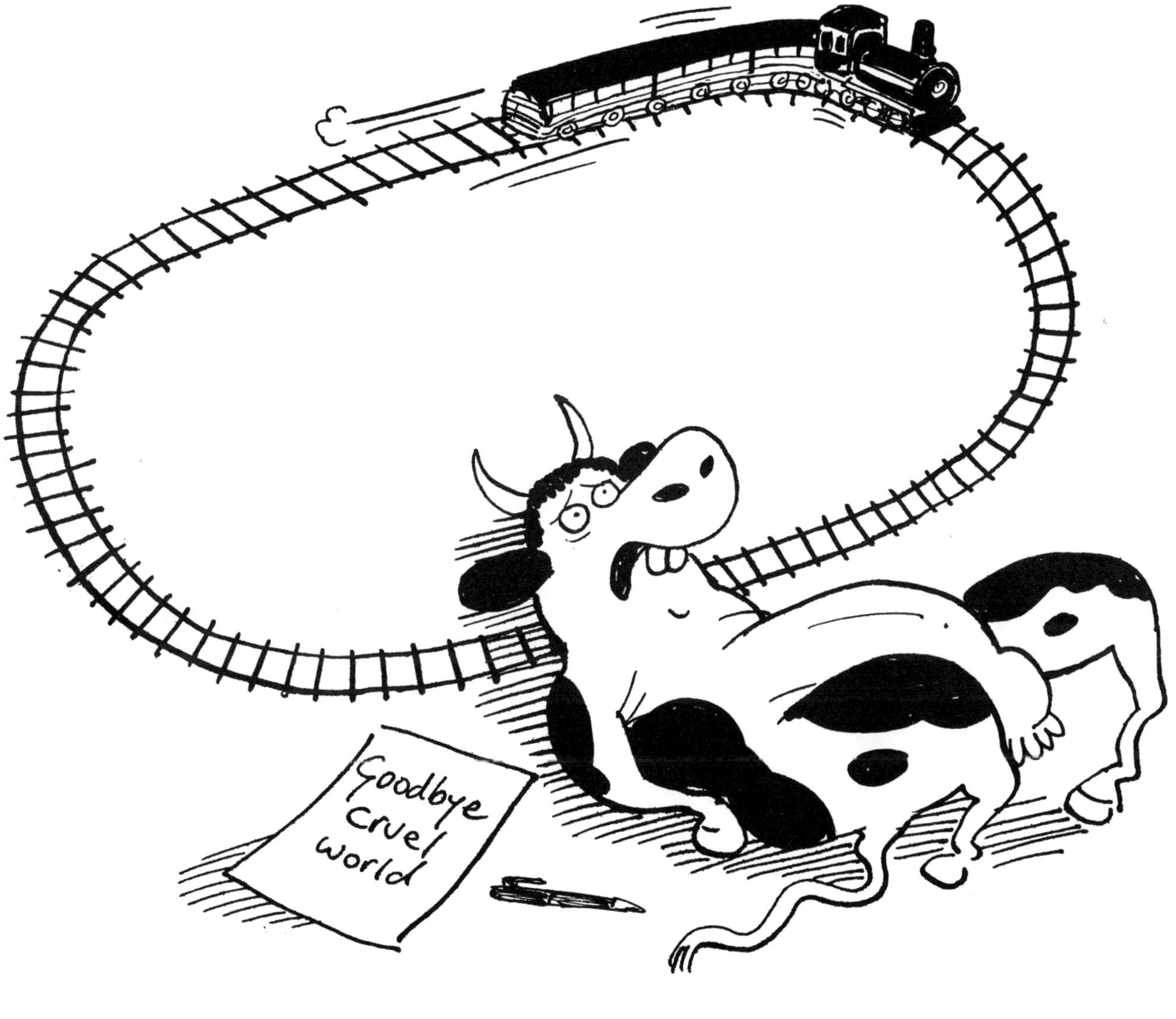
Goodbye
cruel
world

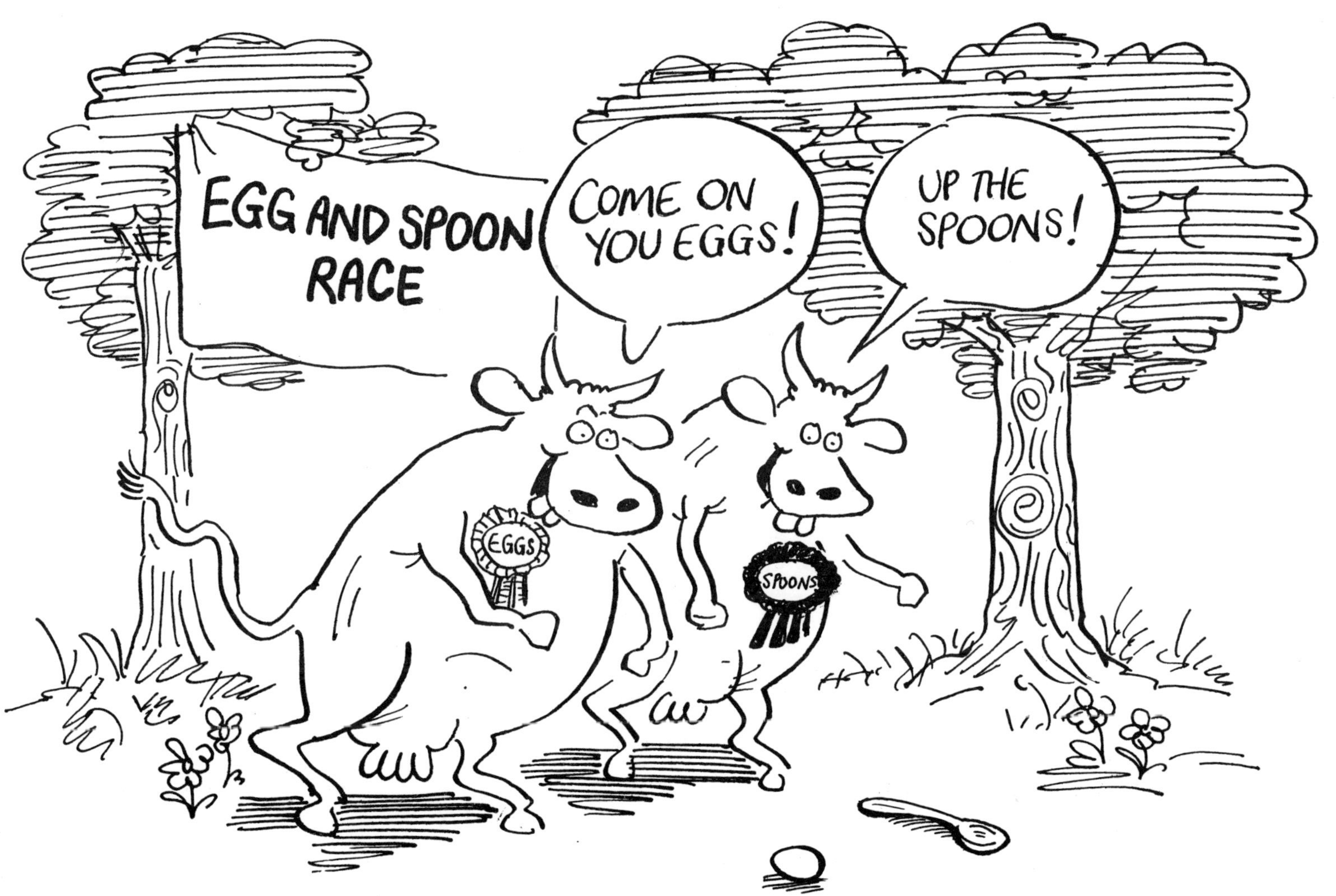
EGG AND SPOON RACE
COME ON YOU EGGS!
UP THE SPOONS!
EGGS
SPOONS

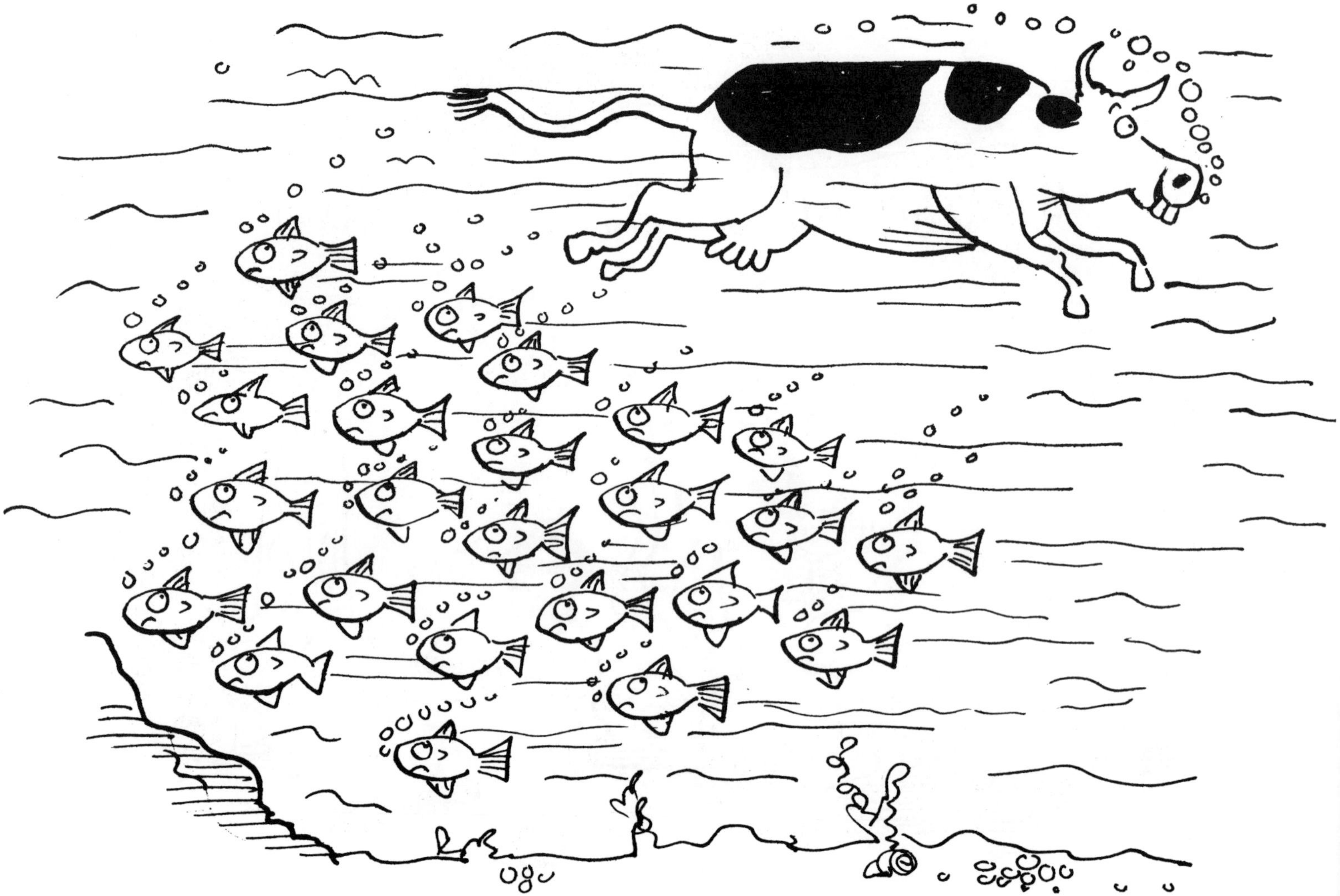

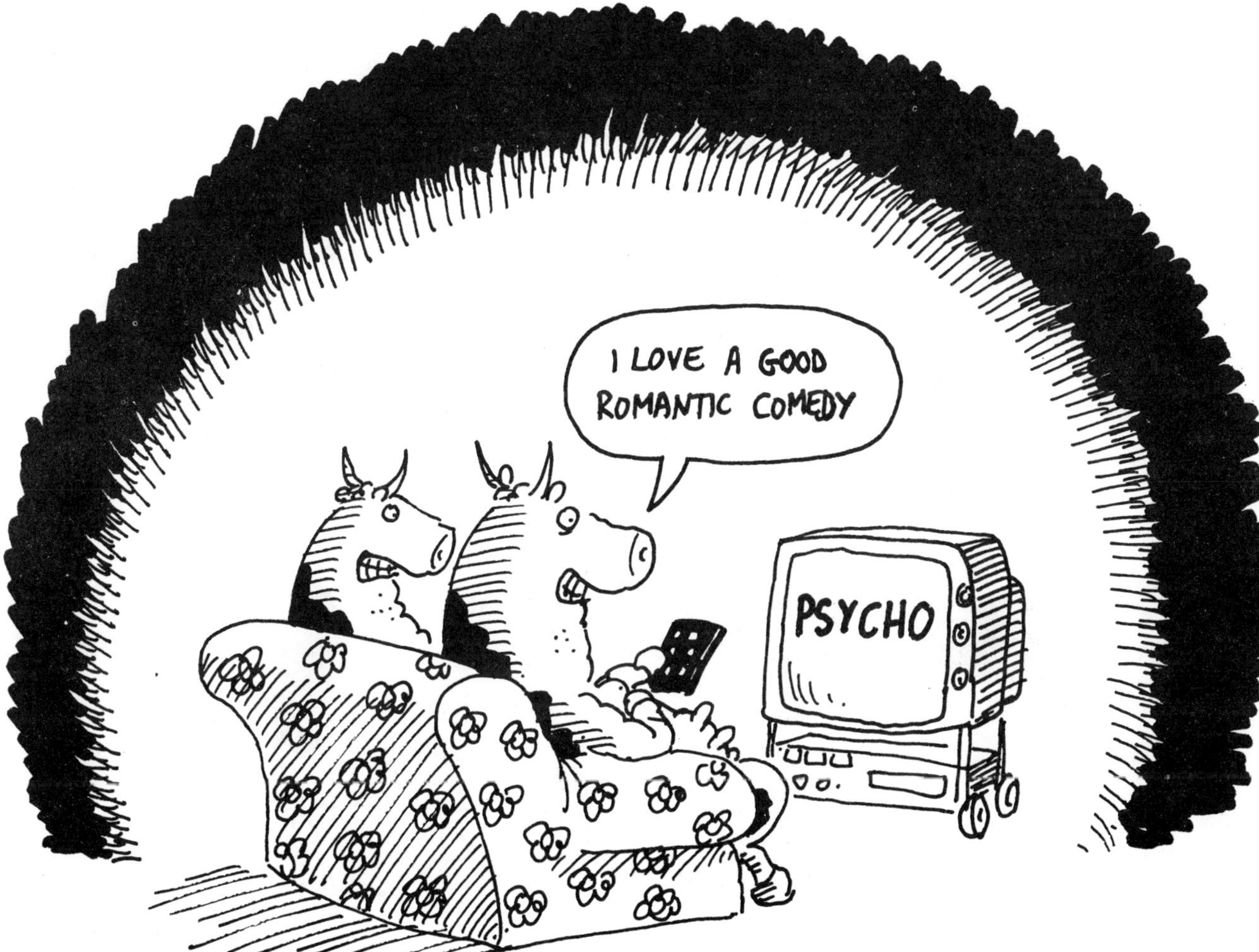
I LOVE A GOOD ROMANTIC COMEDY
PSYCHO

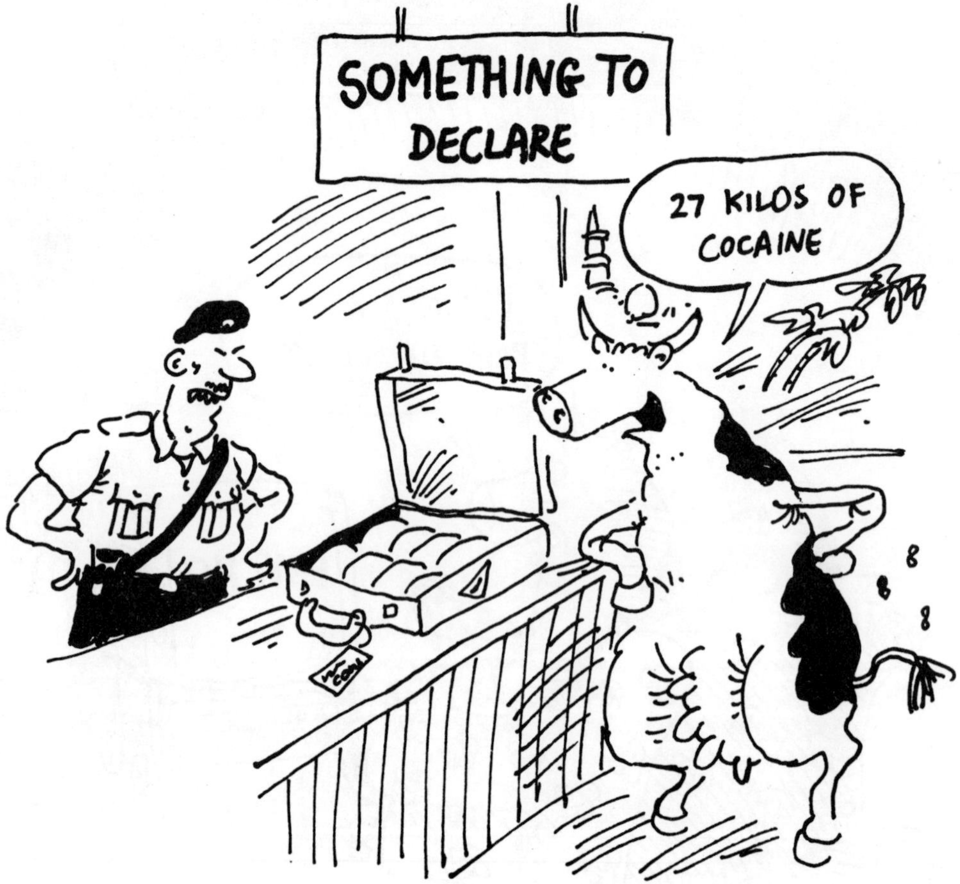
SOMETHING TO DECLARE
27 KILOS OF COCAINE

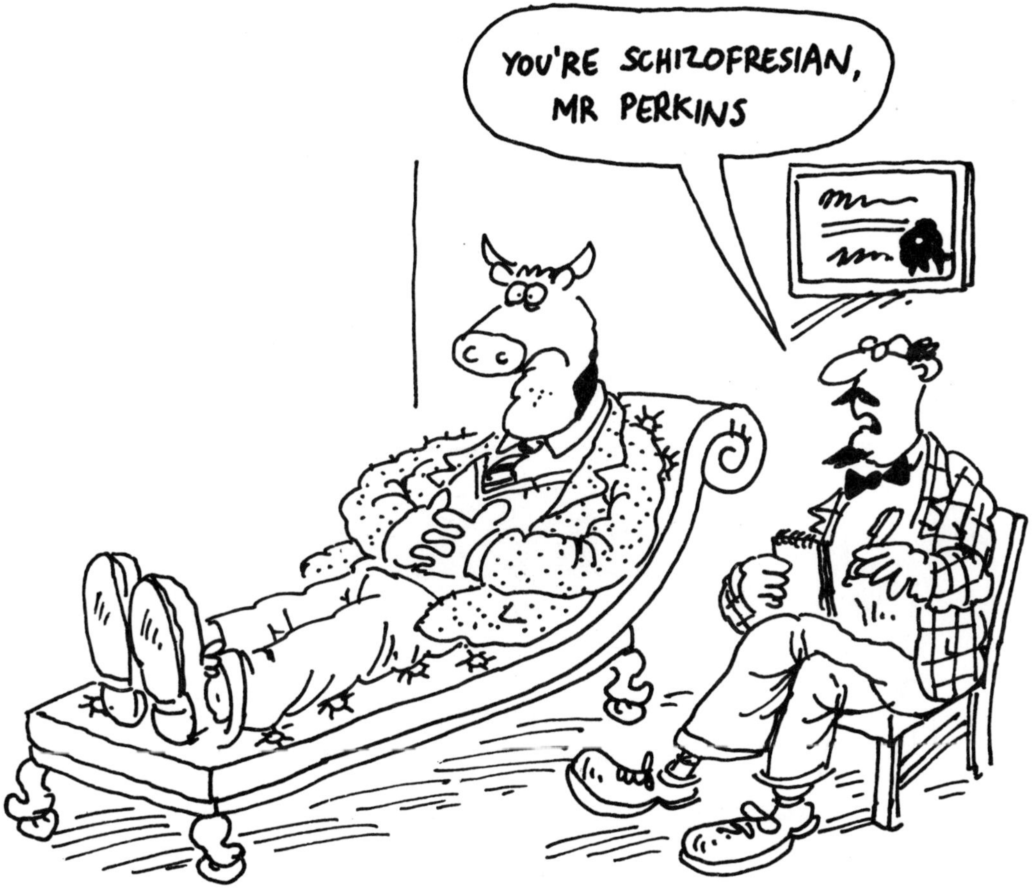
YOU'RE SCHIZOFRESIAN, MR PERKINS

MOONA LISA

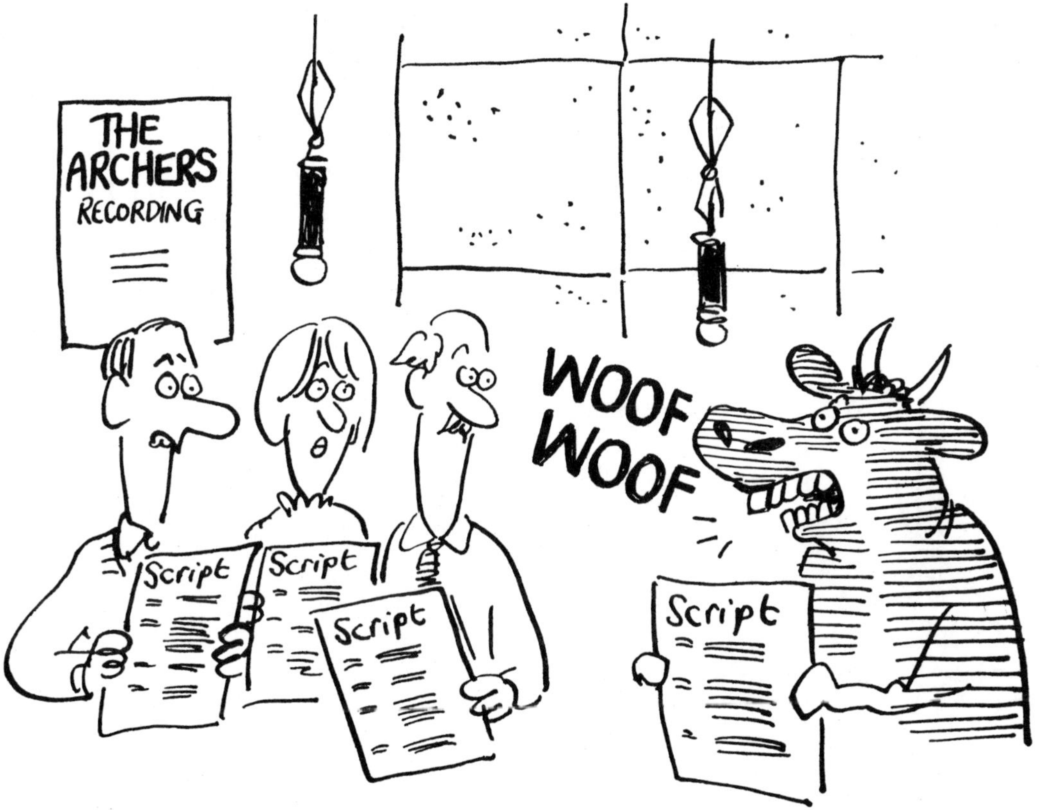
THE ARCHERS
RECORDING
WOOF
WOOF
Script
Script
Script
Script

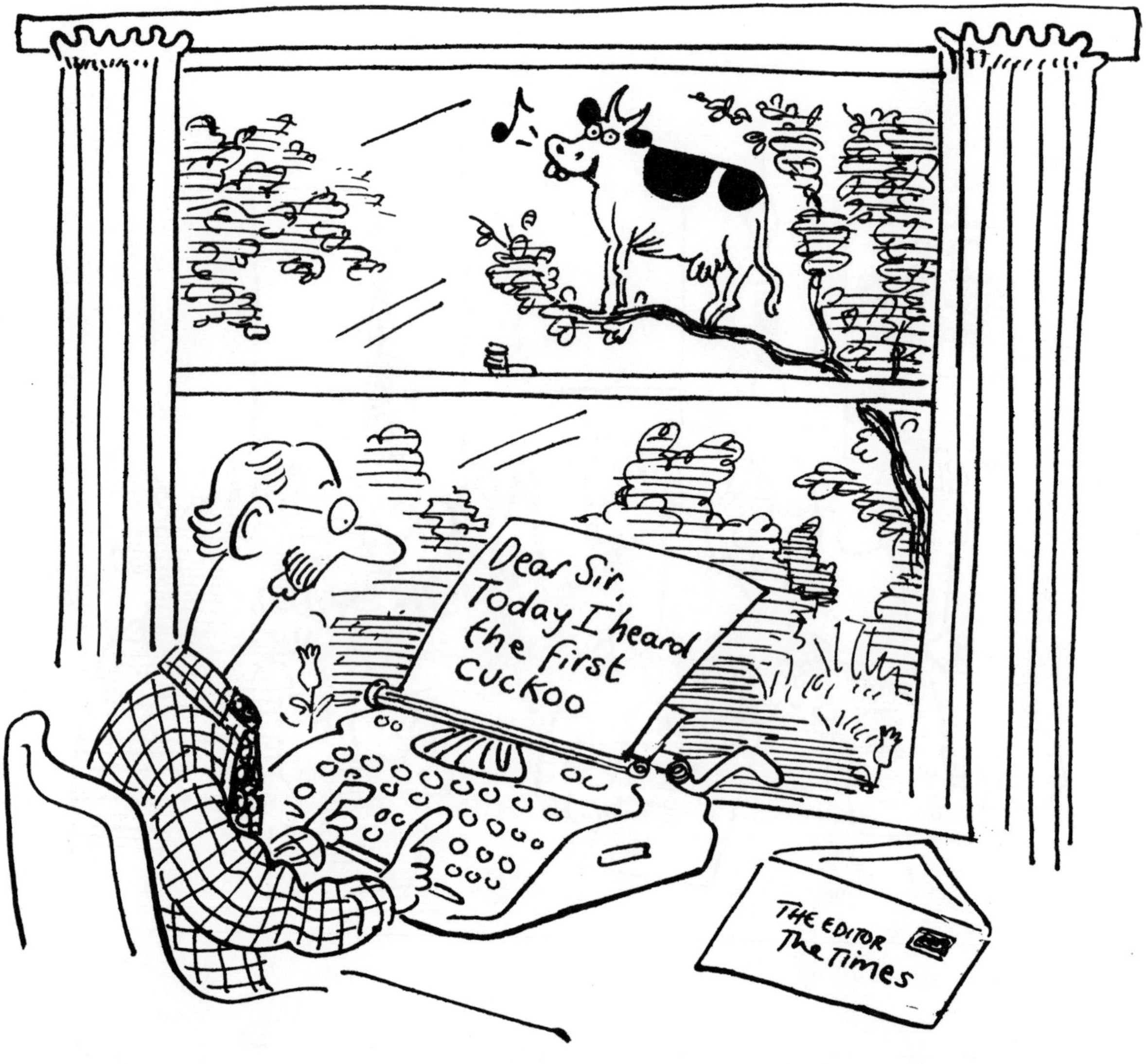
Dear Sir,
Today I heard the first cuckoo
THE EDITOR
The Times

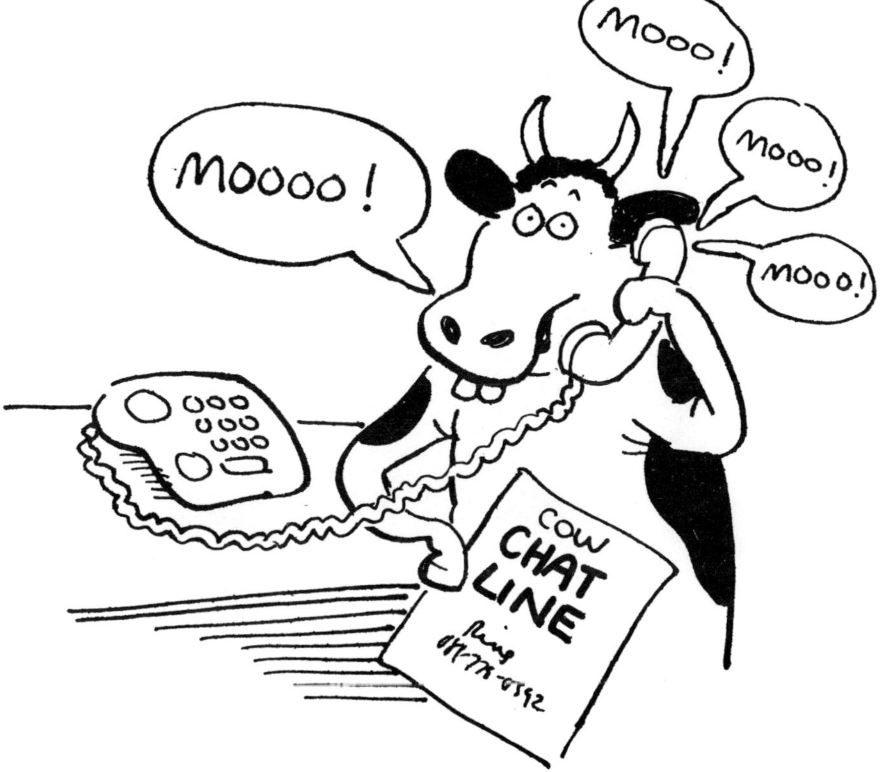
Moooo!
Mooo!
Mooo!
Mooo!
COW
CHAT
LINE
Ring

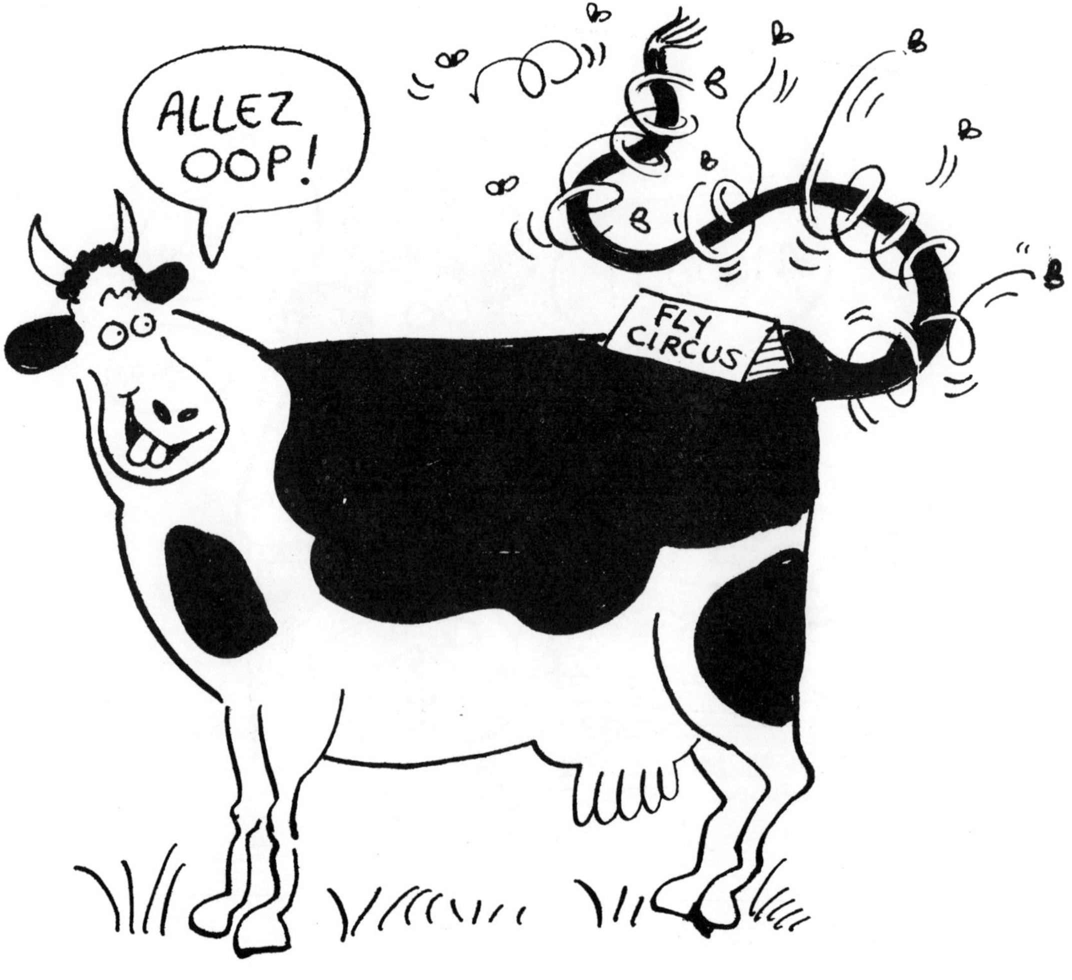
ALLEZ OOP!
FLY CIRCUS

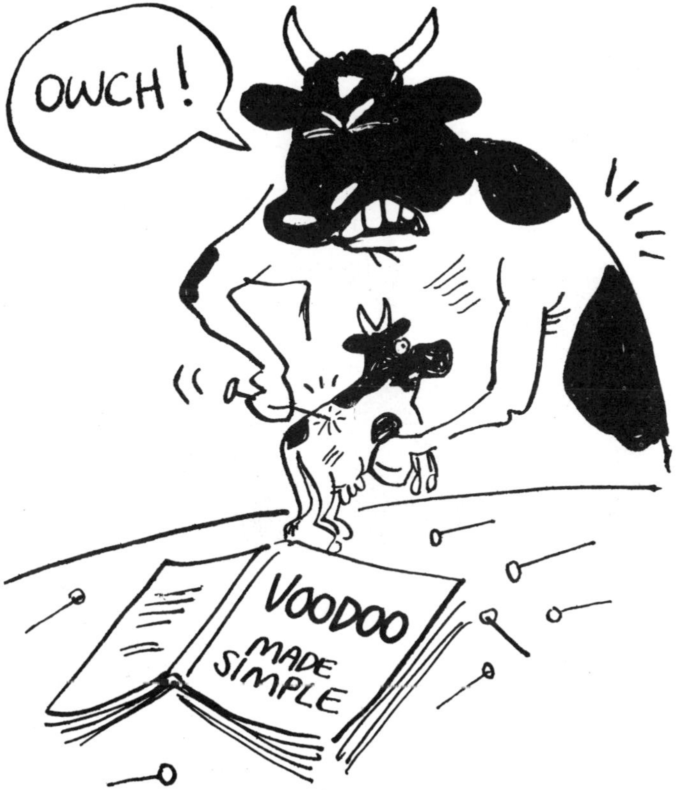
OWCH!
VOODOO
MADE SIMPLE

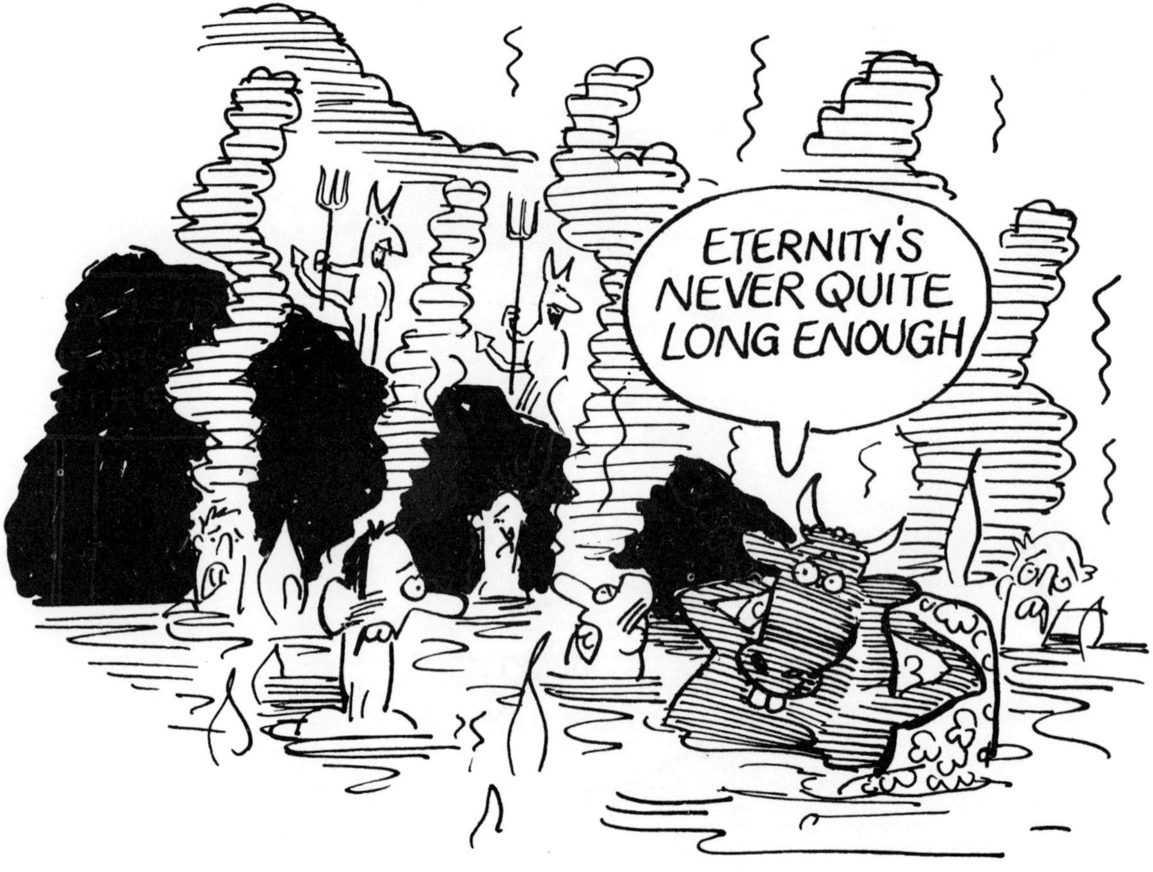
ETERNITY'S NEVER QUITE LONG ENOUGH

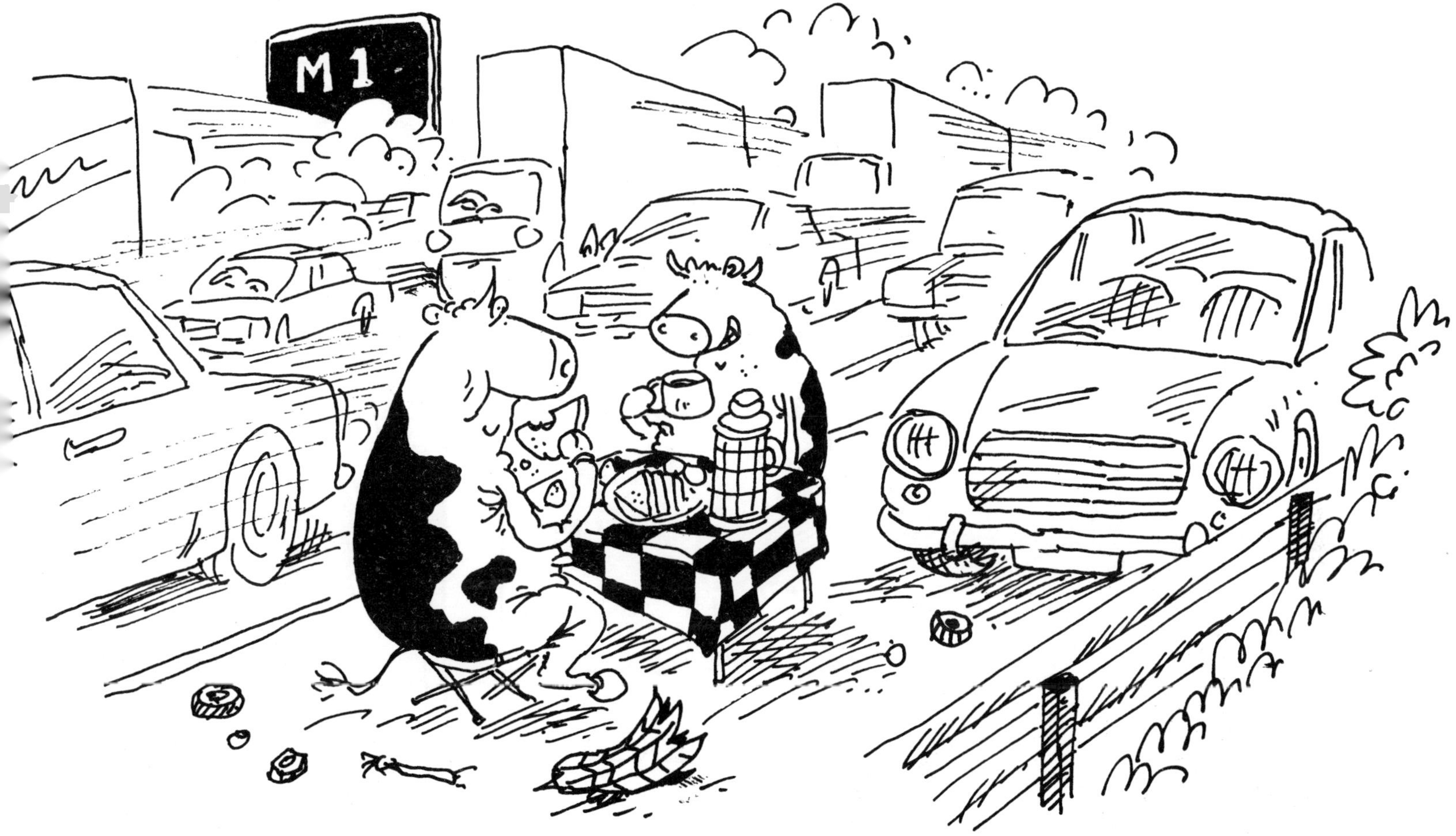
M1

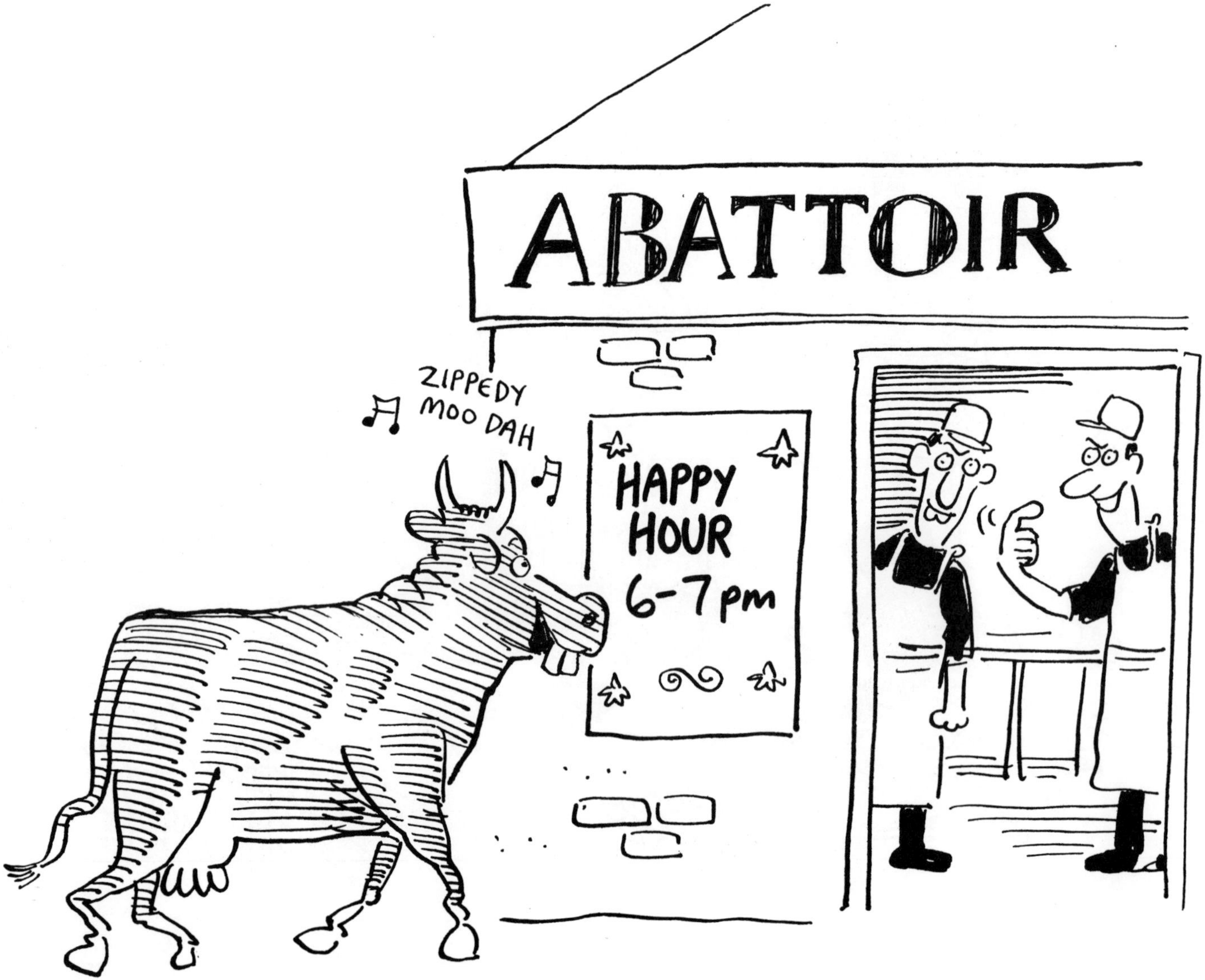
ABATTOIR
ZIPPEDY MOO DAH
HAPPY HOUR 6-7pm

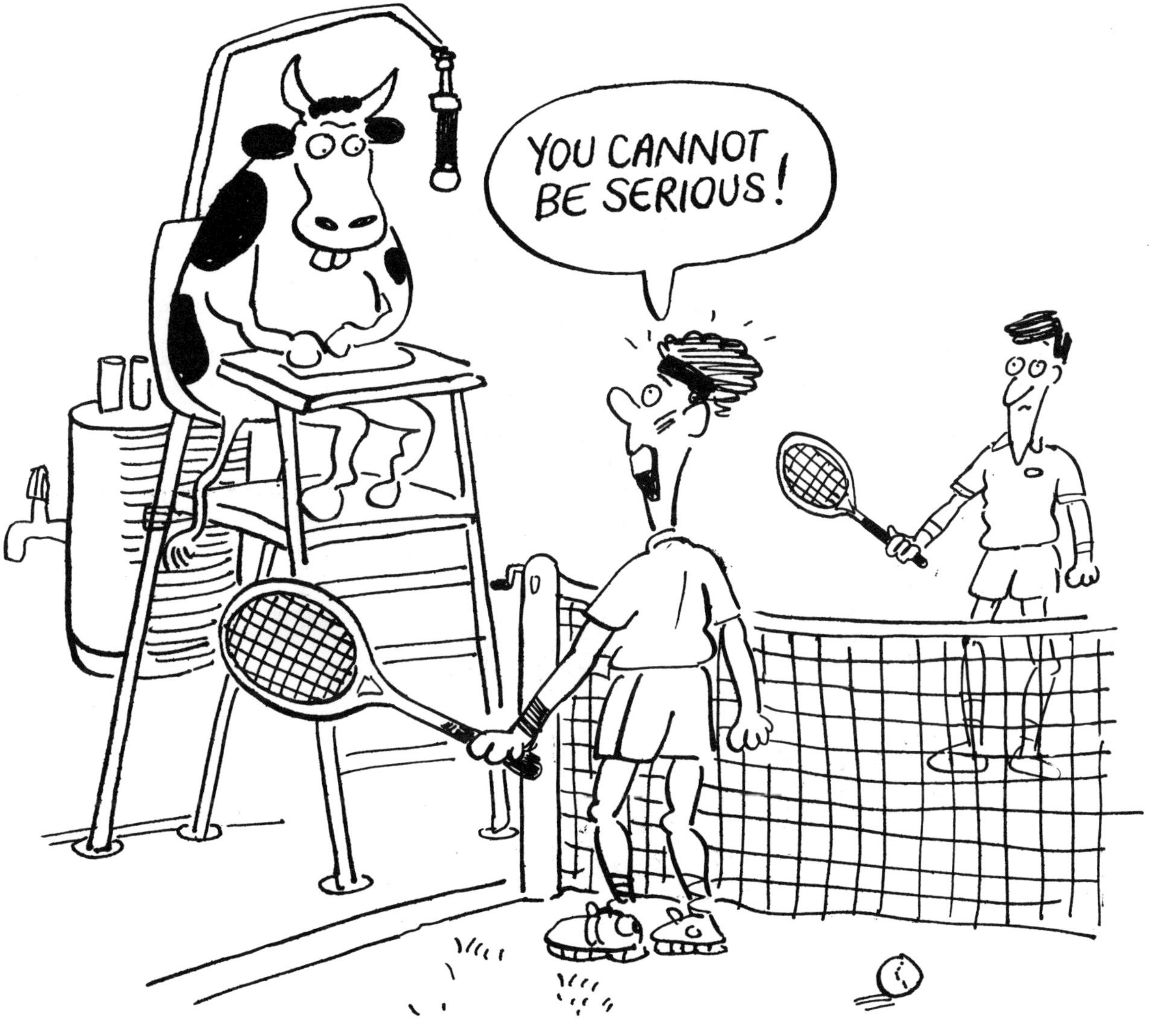
YOU CANNOT BE SERIOUS!

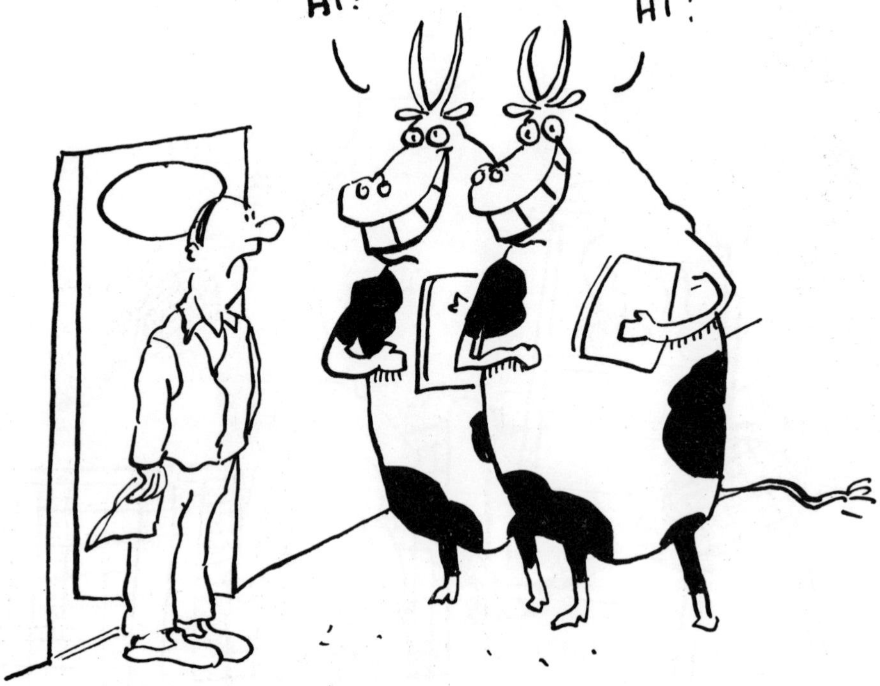
HI!
HI!

MOO-NIES

MOOOOOON RIVER...

BUTCHER SHOP QUARTETTE.

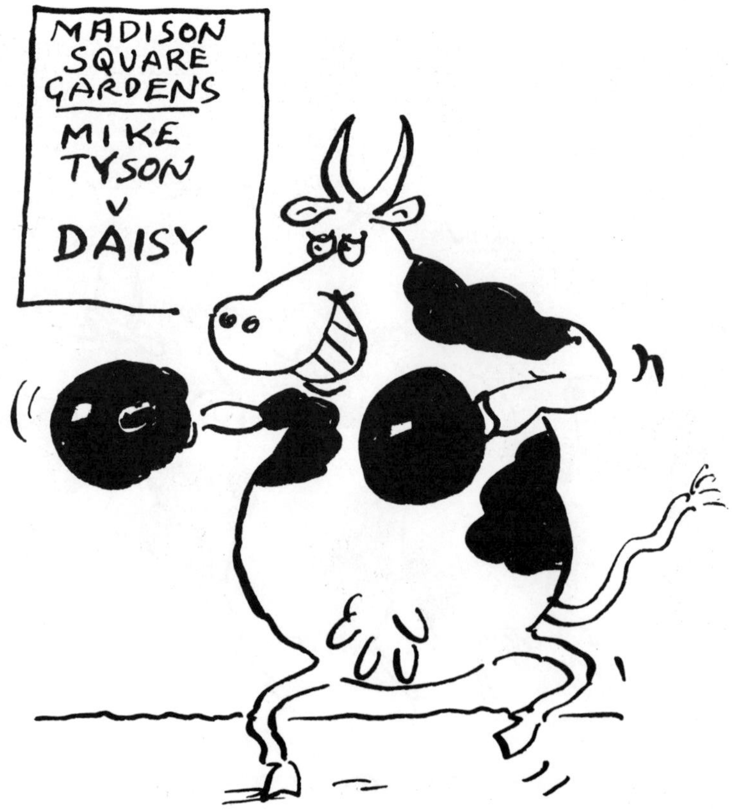
MADISON
SQUARE
GARDENS
MIKE
TYSON
v
DAISY

FIGHTING MAD

MOO-NLIGHTING.

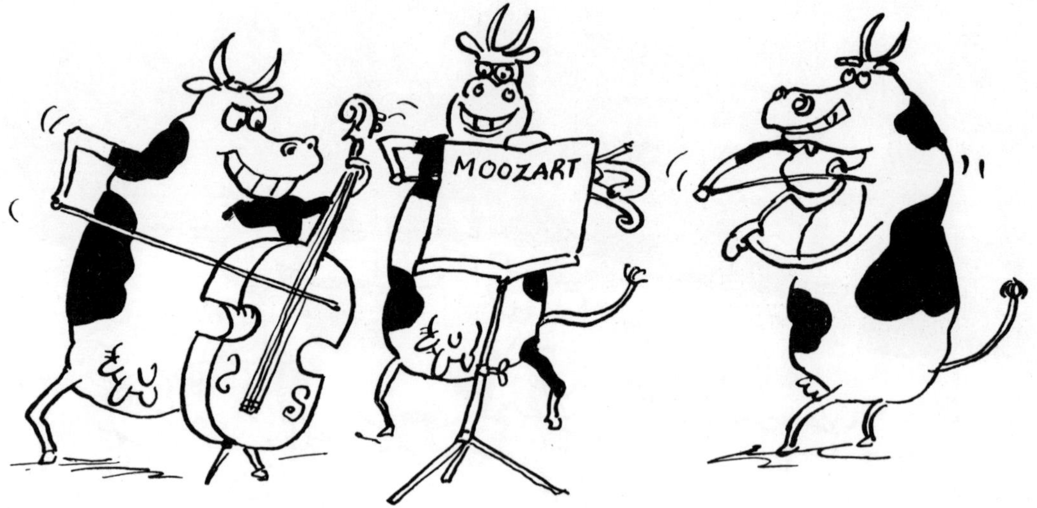
MOOZART

CHAMBER MOO-SIC.

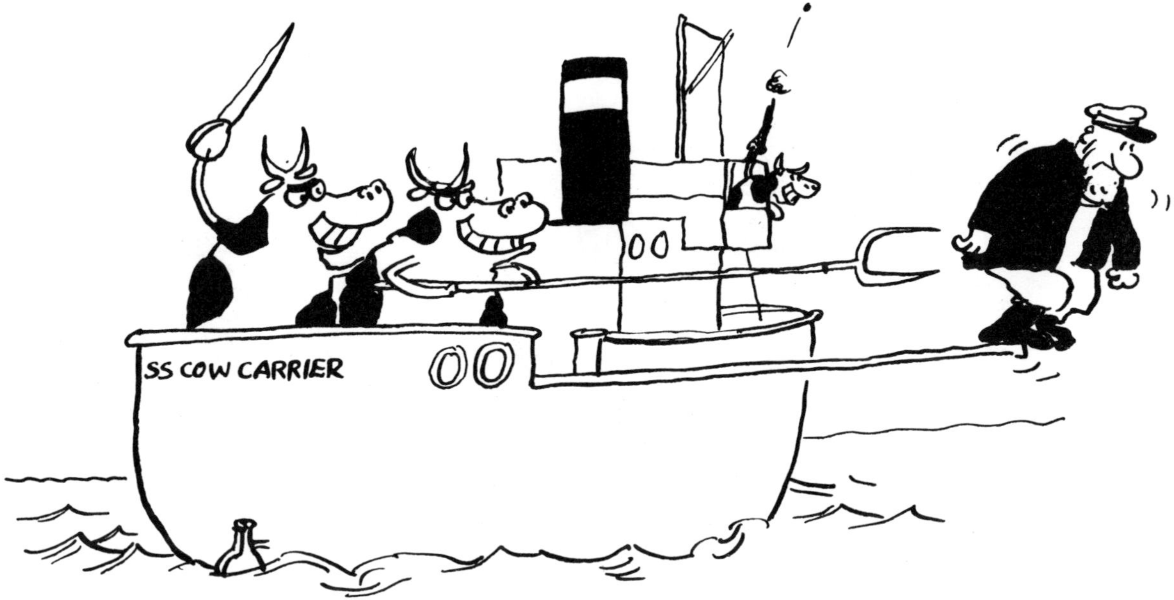
SS COW CARRIER

MOO-TINEERS.

MOO- SKETEERS

MOO-CHING ABOUT

MOO-NING.

MOO-NICIPAL

MOO-LIN ROUGE.

MOO-TATION

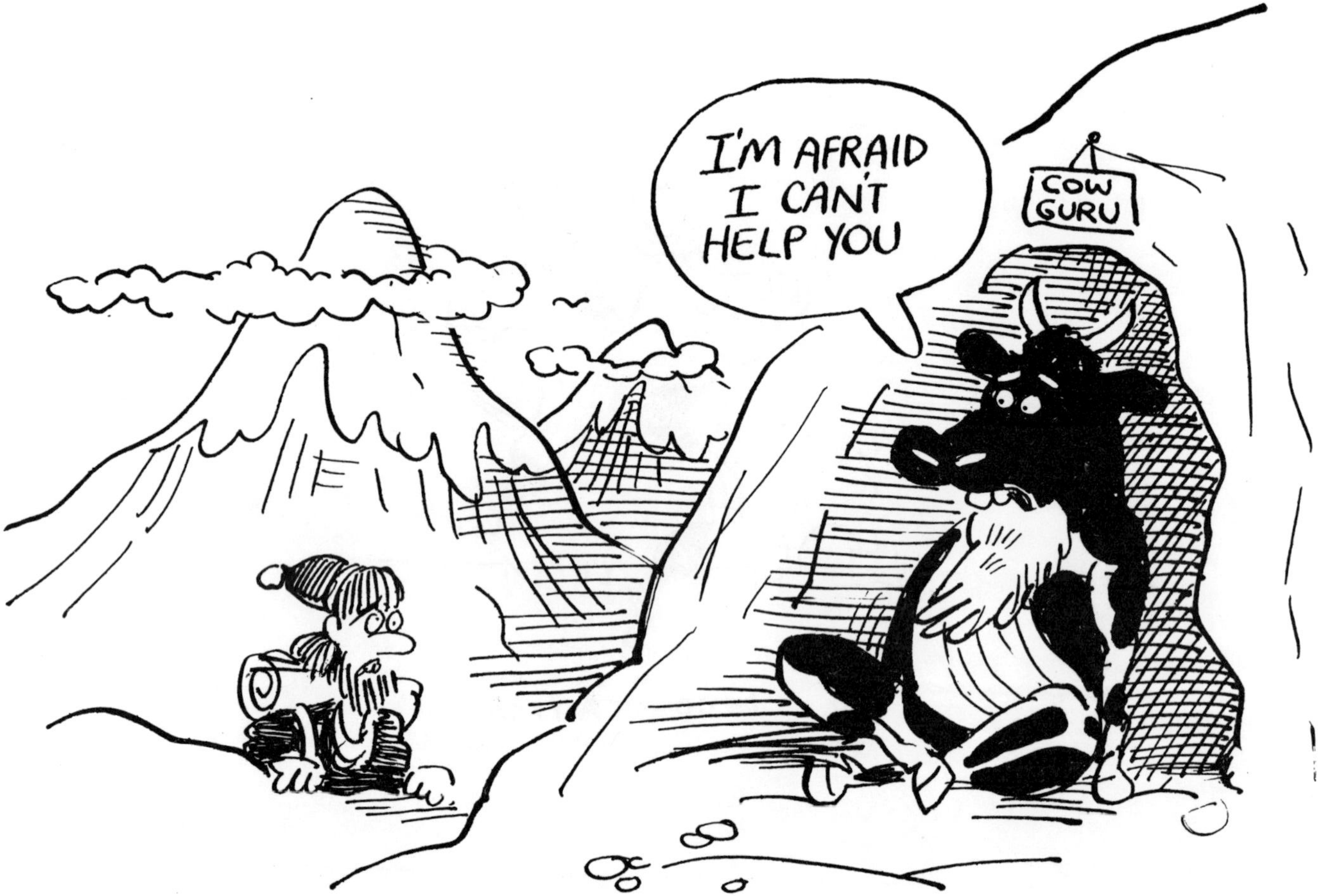
I'M AFRAID I CAN'T HELP YOU
COW GURU

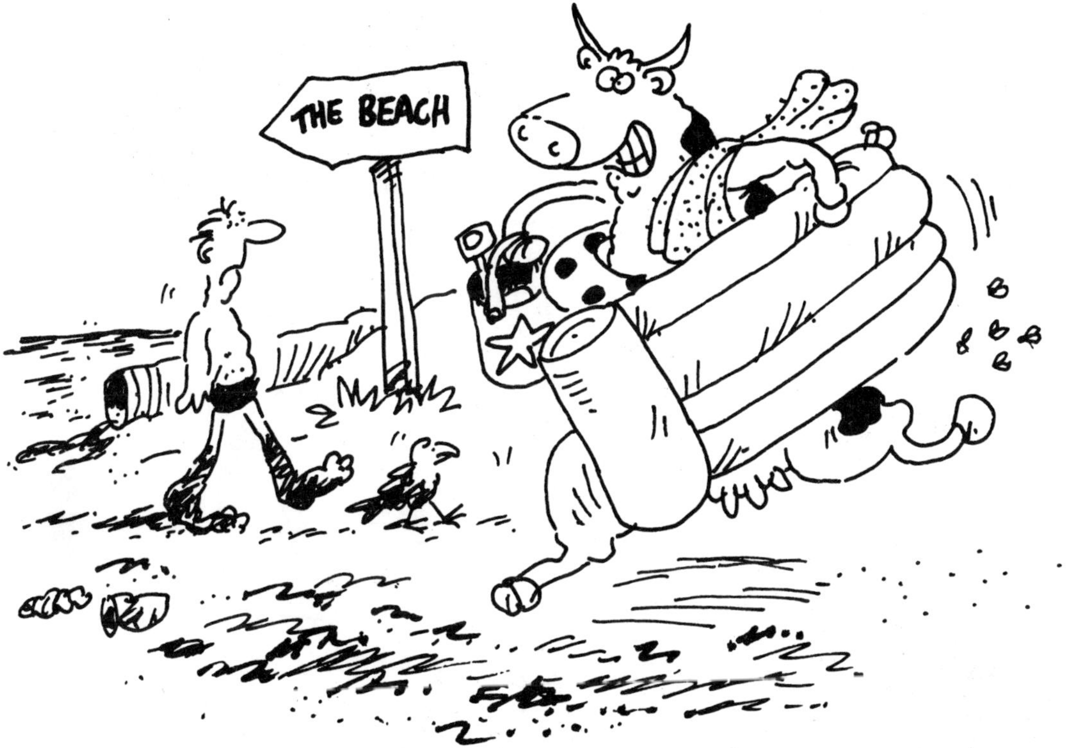
THE BEACH

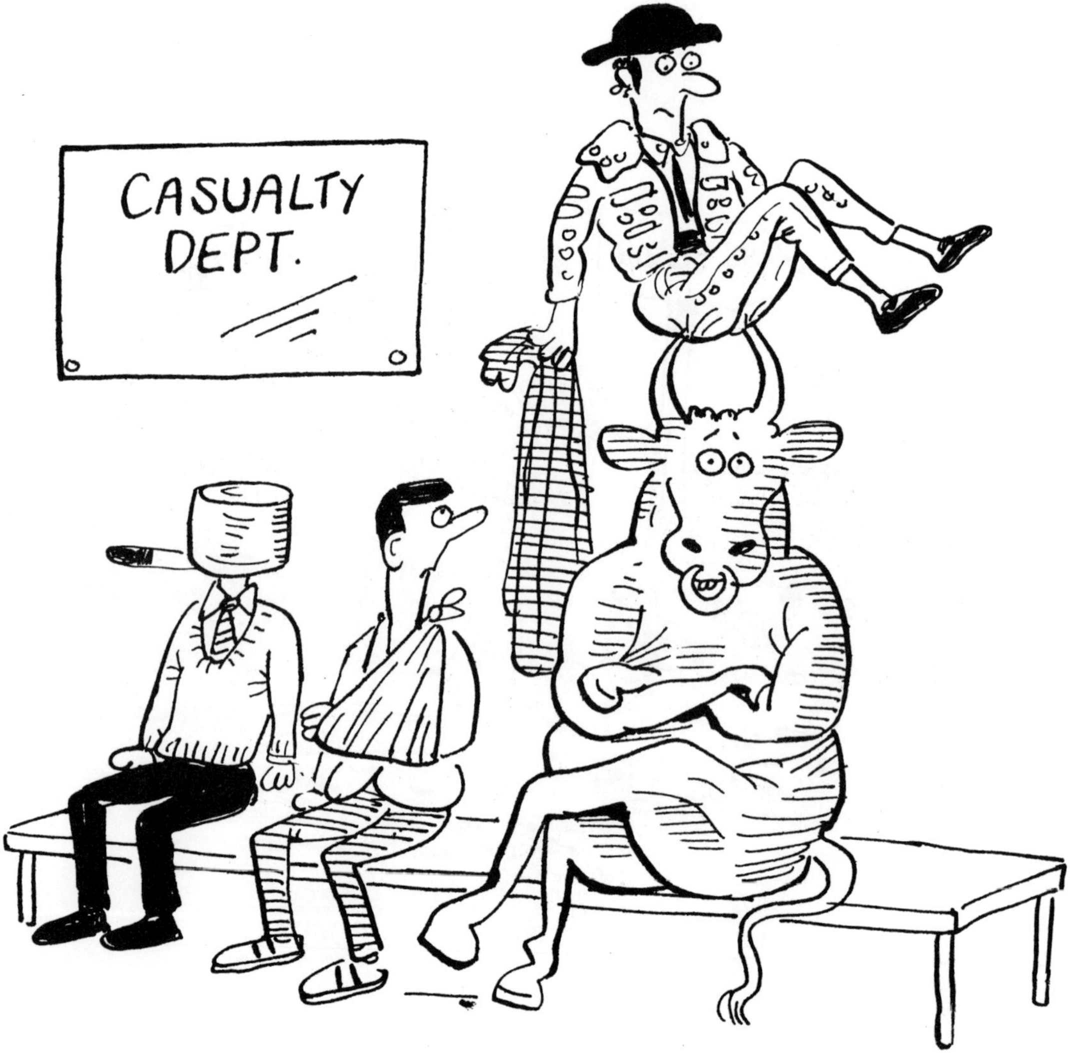
CASUALTY
DEPT.

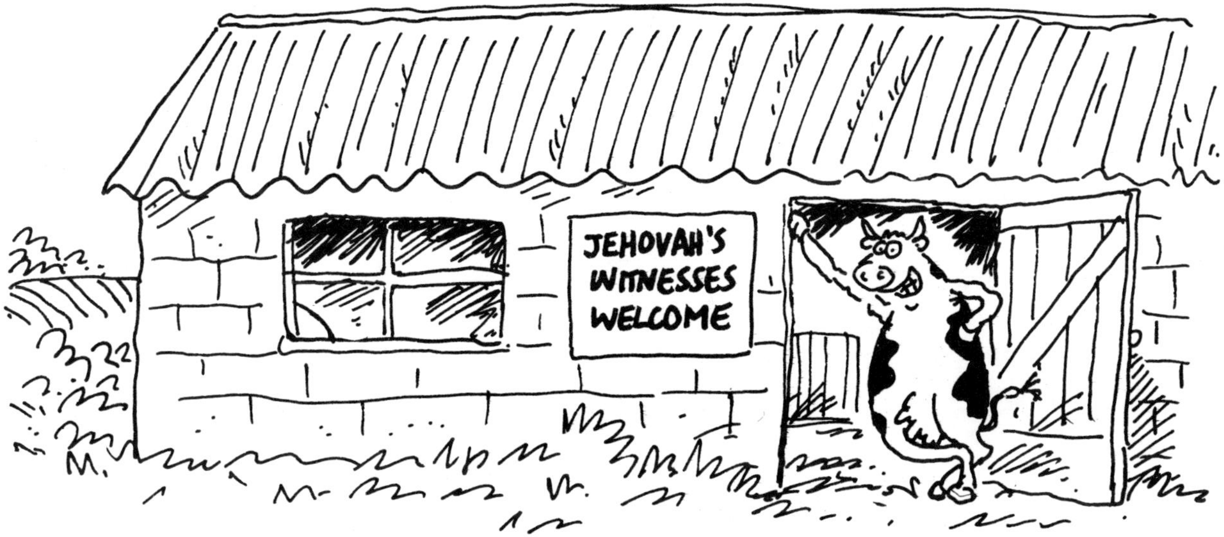
JEHOVAH'S
WITNESSES
WELCOME

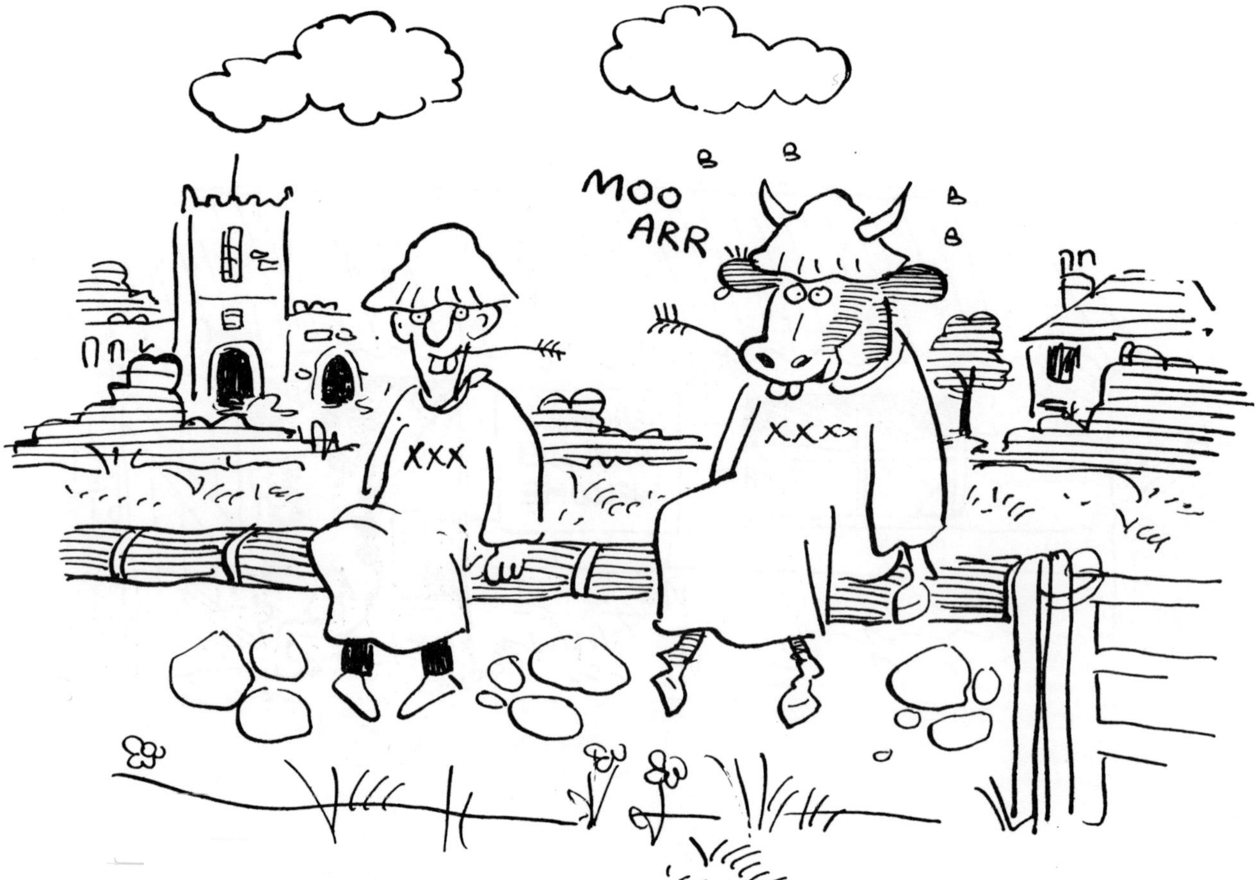

MOO
ARR
XXX
XXXX

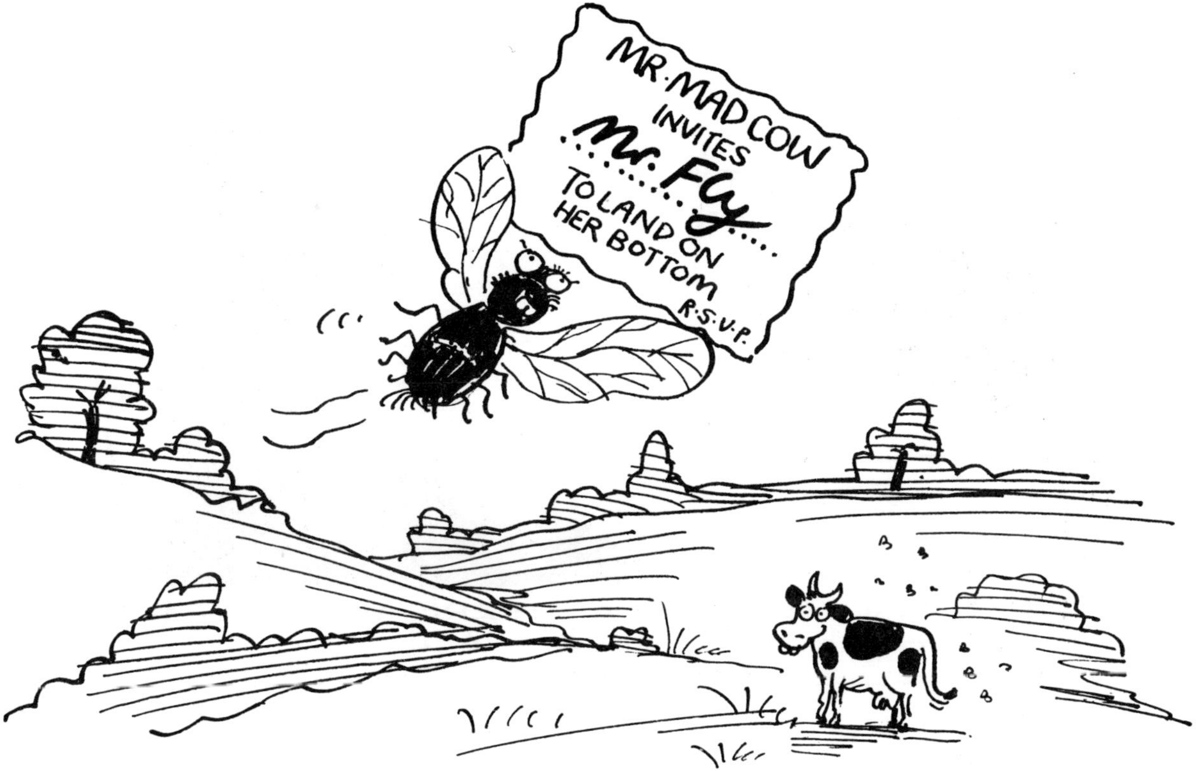
MR. MAD COW
INVITES
Mr. Fly
TO LAND ON
HER BOTTOM
R.S.V.P.

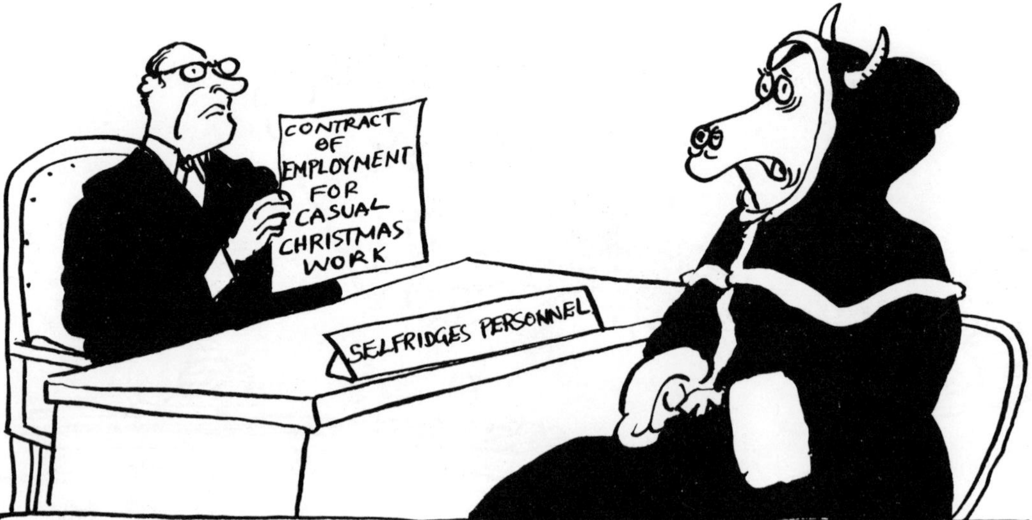
CONTRACT
OF
EMPLOYMENT
FOR
CASUAL
CHRISTMAS
WORK
SELFRIDGES PERSONNEL

DAISY DISCOVERED THAT THERE WAS IN FACT A SANITY CLAUSE AFTER ALL.

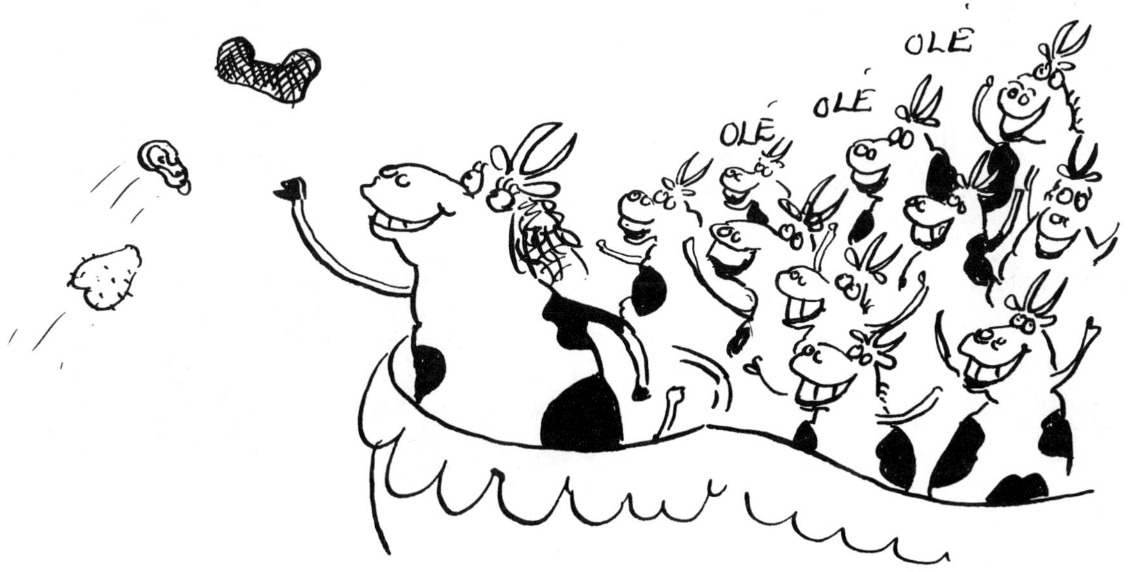
OLÉ
OLÉ
OLÉ

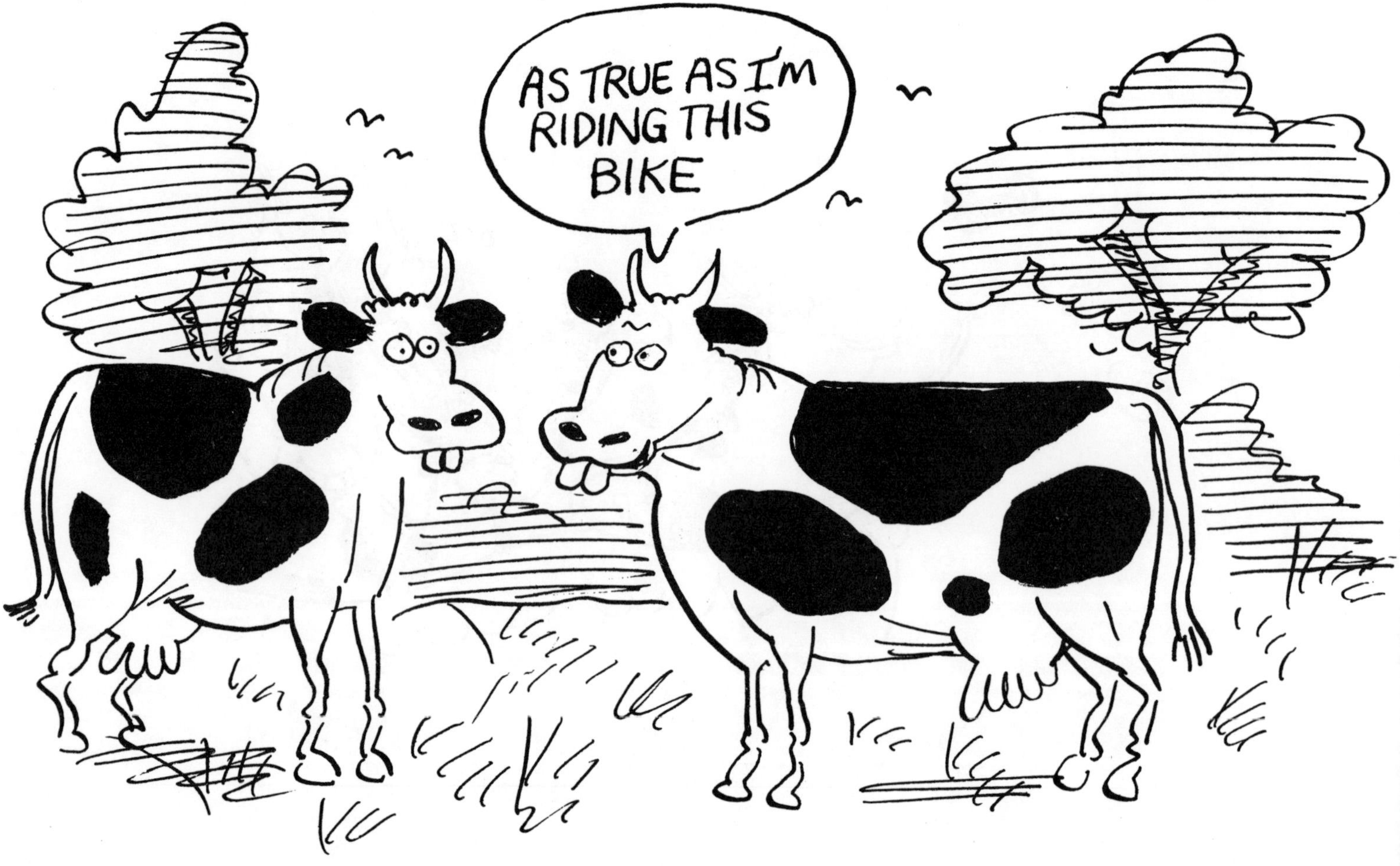
AS TRUE AS I'M RIDING THIS BIKE

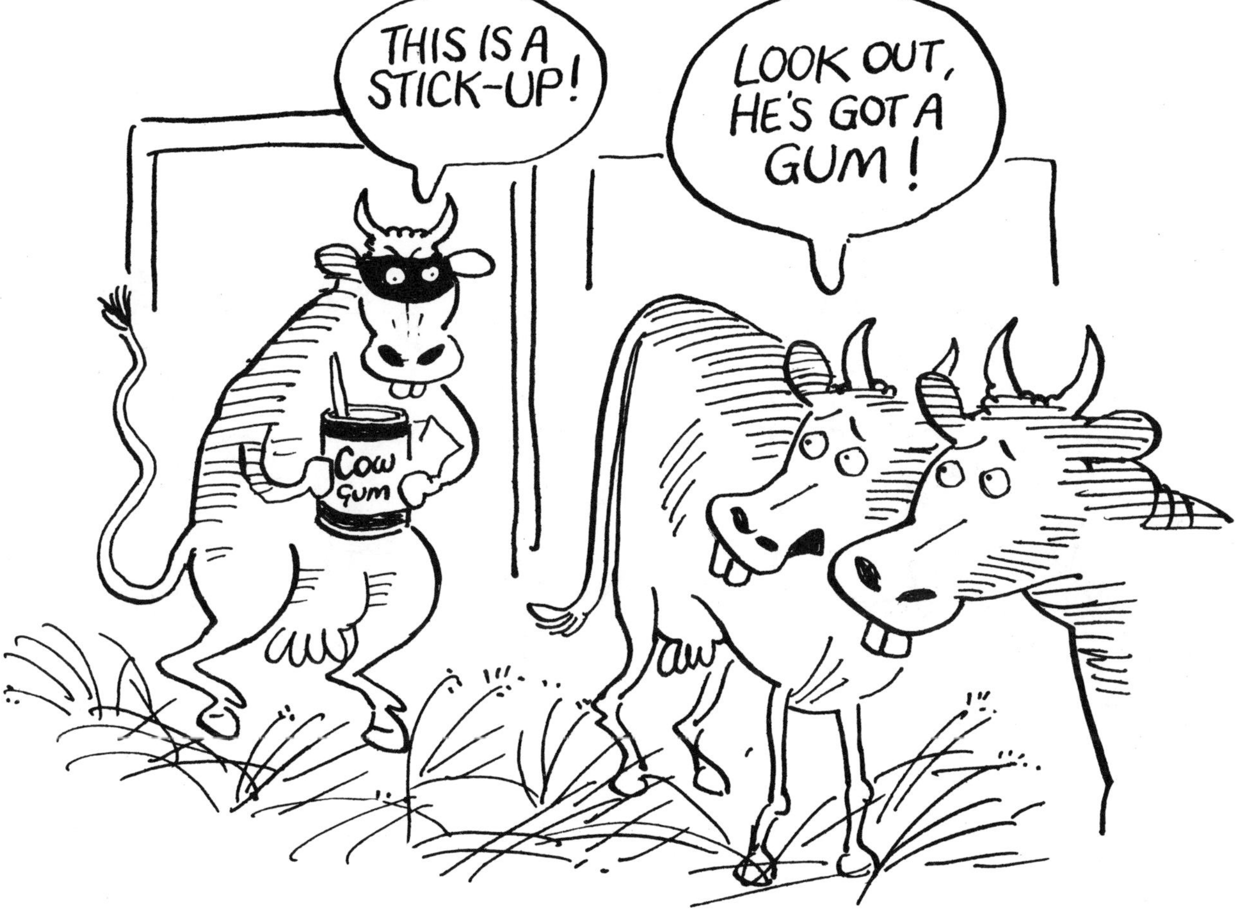
THIS IS A STICK-UP!
LOOK OUT, HE'S GOT A GUM!
COW GUM

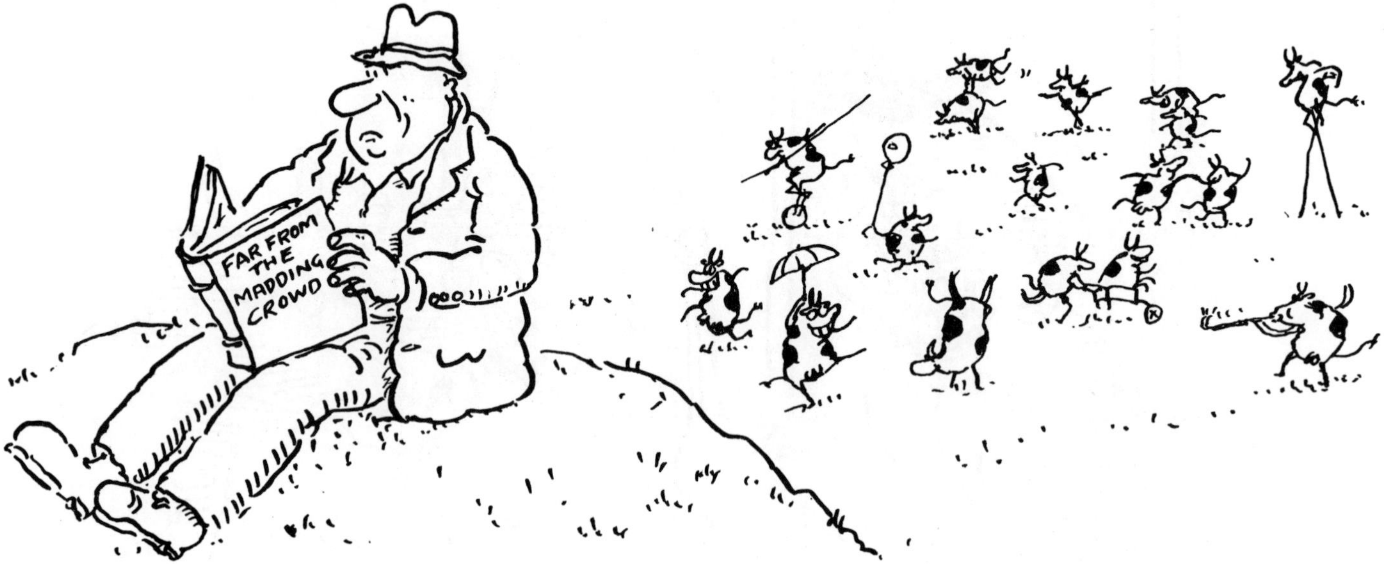
FAR FROM THE MADDING CROWD

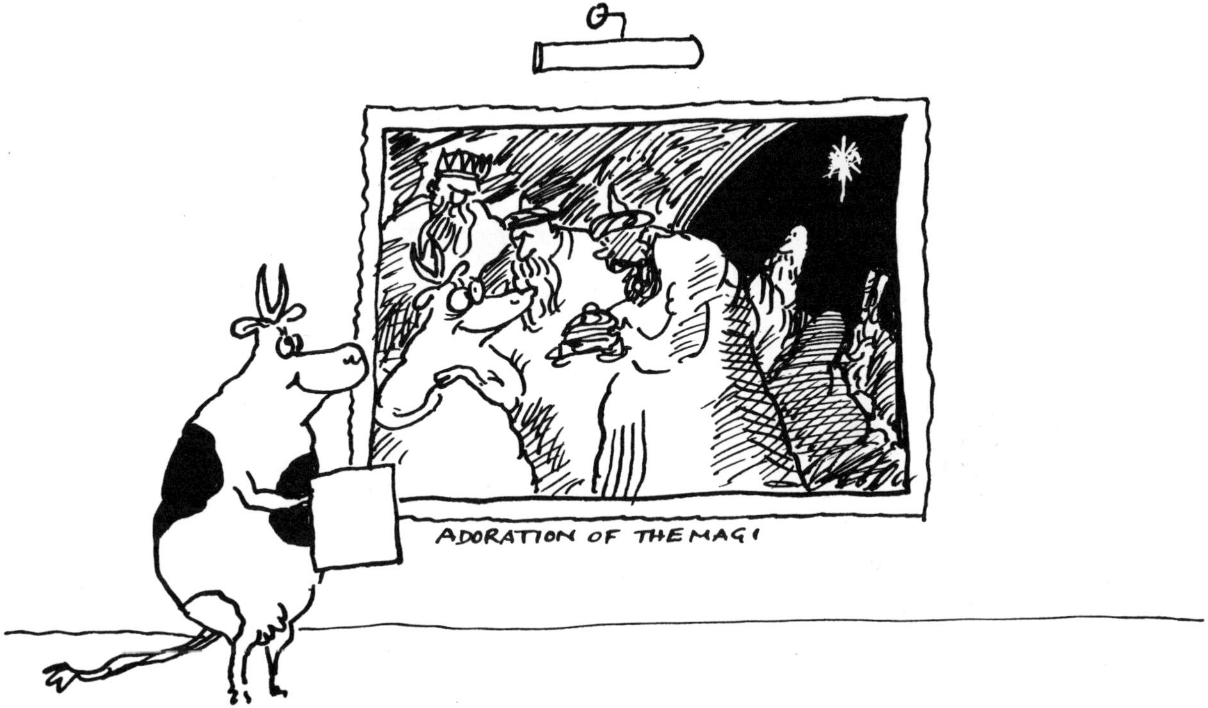
ADORATION OF THE MAGI

LE DEJEUNER SUR L'HERBE.

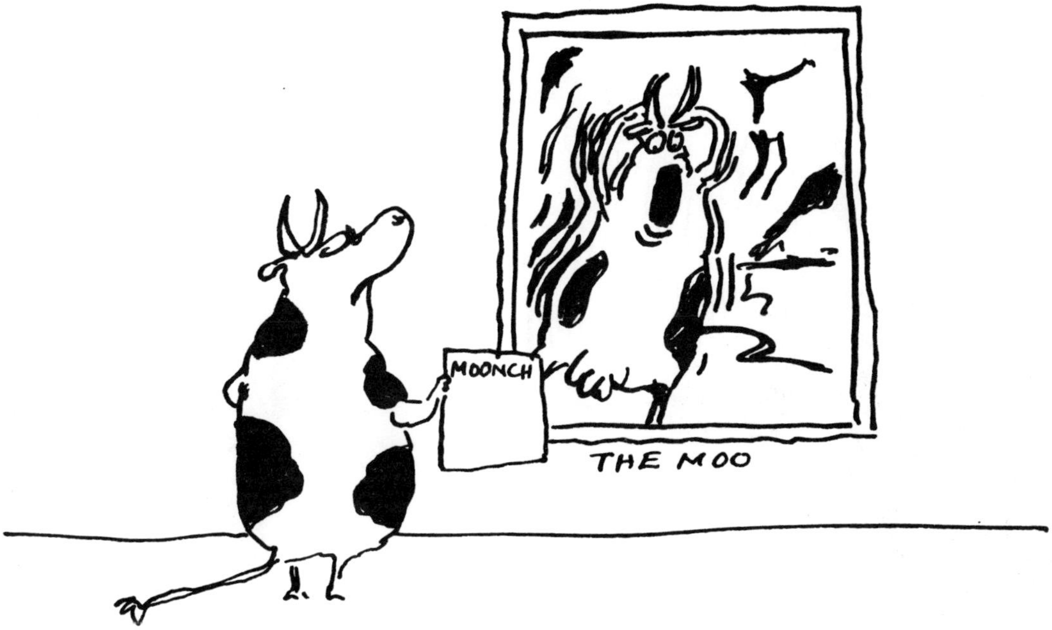
MOONCH
THE MOO

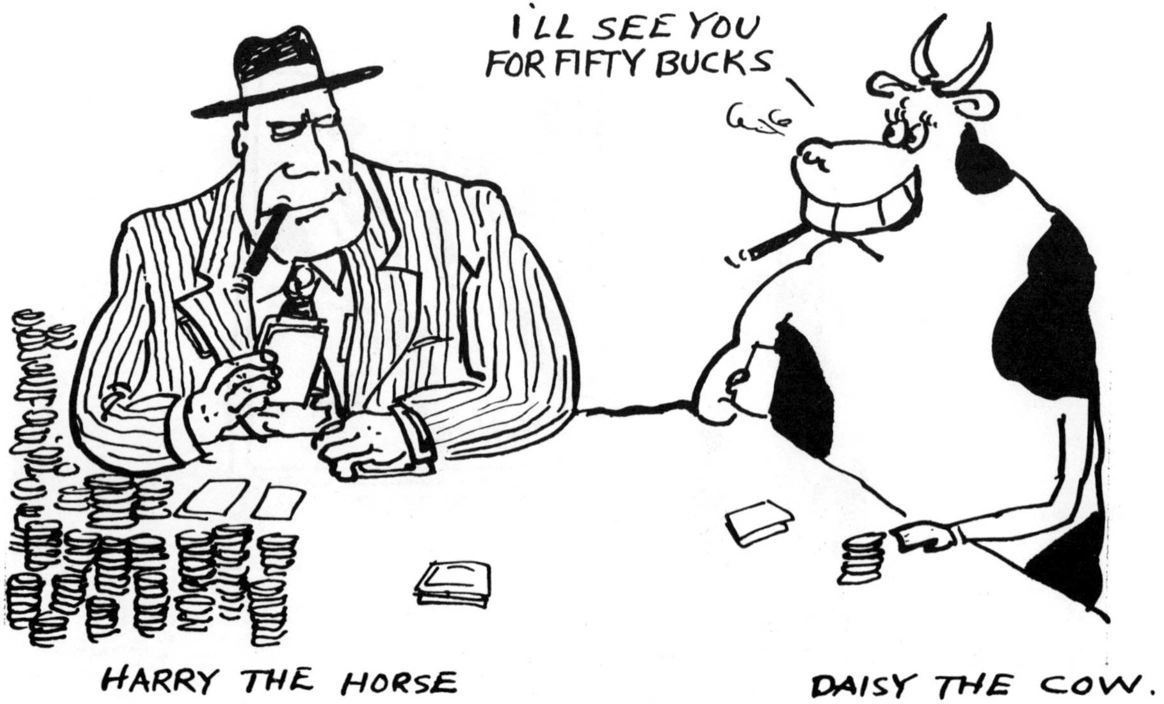
I'LL SEE YOU FOR FIFTY BUCKS
HARRY THE HORSE
DAISY THE COW.

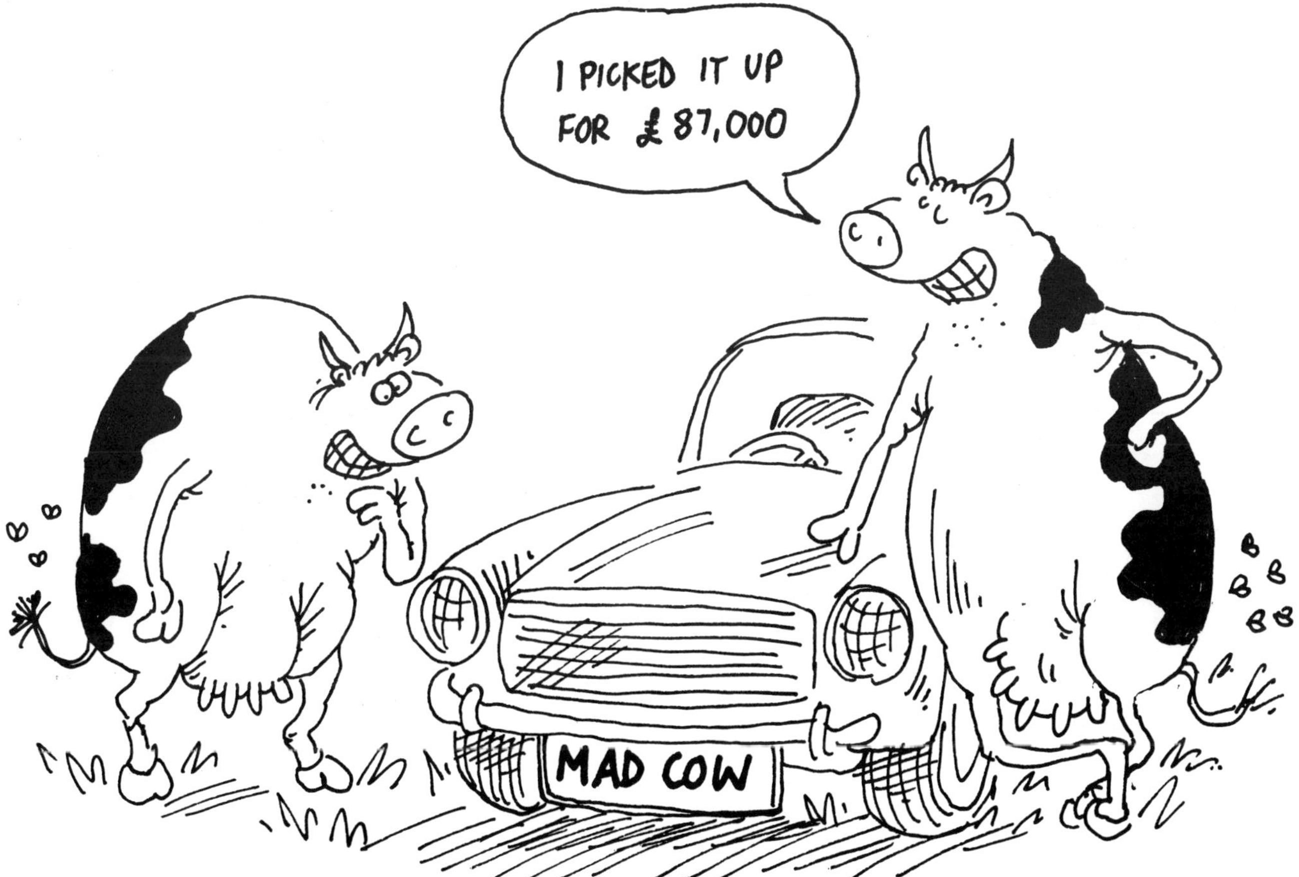
I PICKED IT UP FOR £87,000
MAD COW

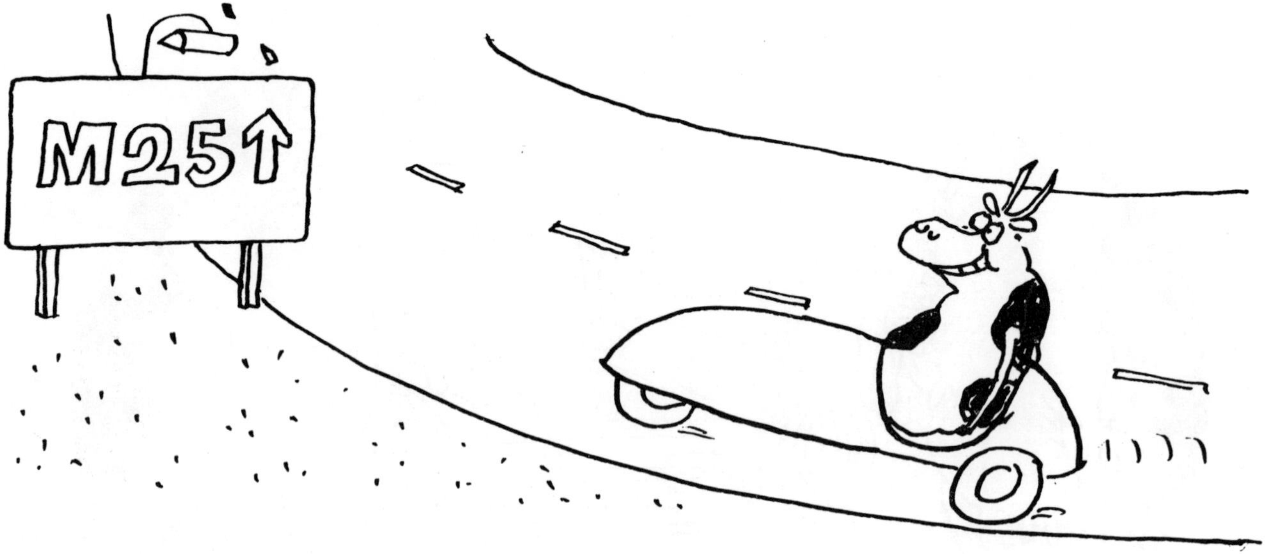
M25↑

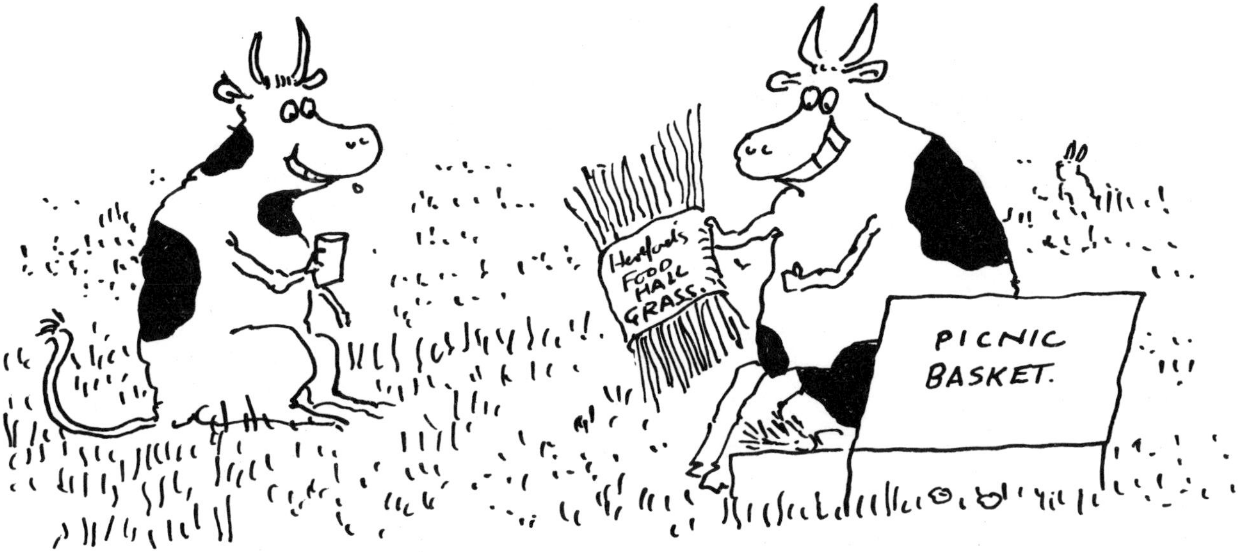
Herefords
FOOD
HALL
GRASS.
PICNIC
BASKET.

... AY-AY-AY · AY-AY CON-GA — AY · AY-AY-AY-AY CON-GA ···

CORN CIRCLES EXPLAINED.

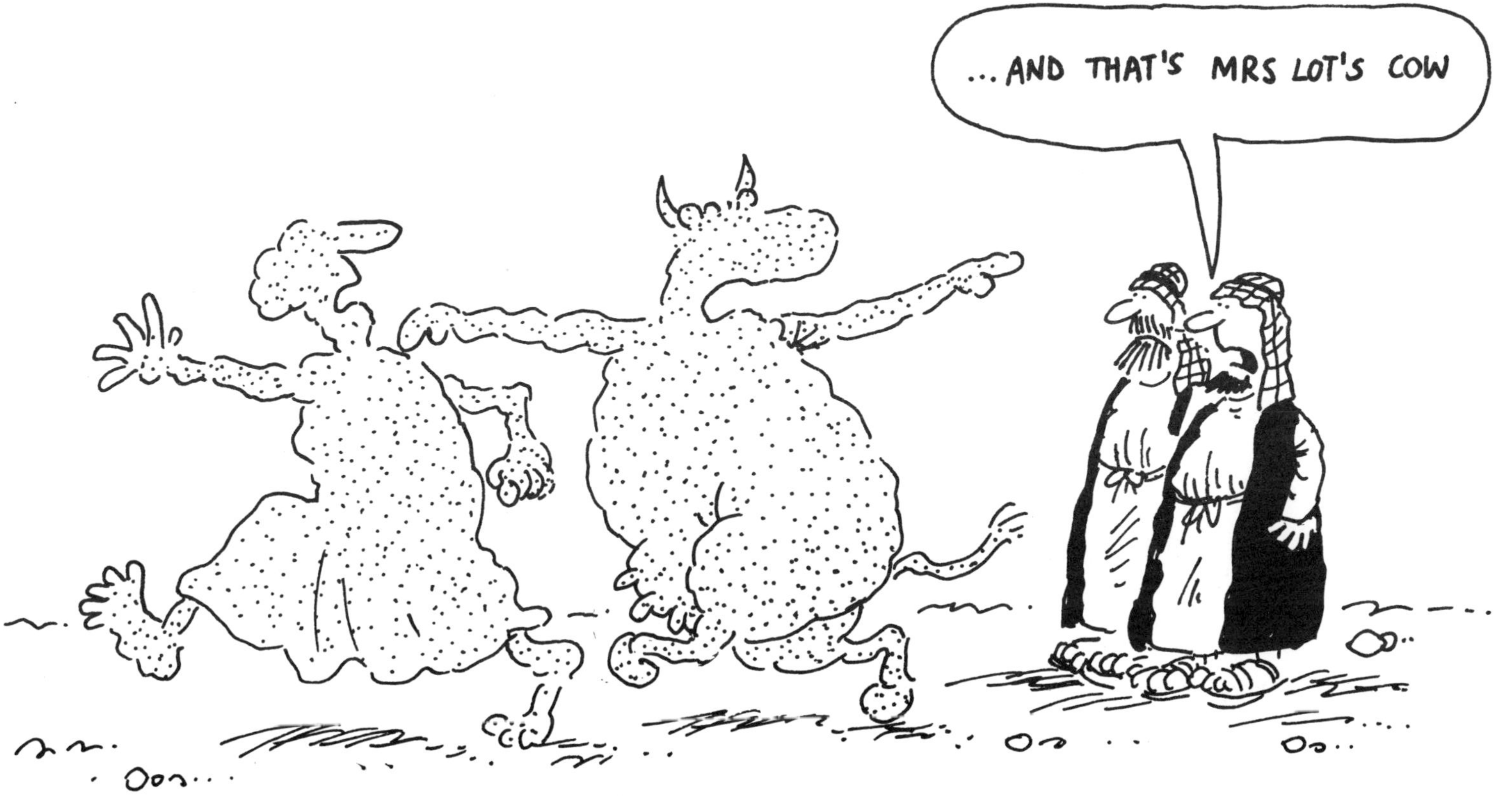
...AND THAT'S MRS LOT'S COW

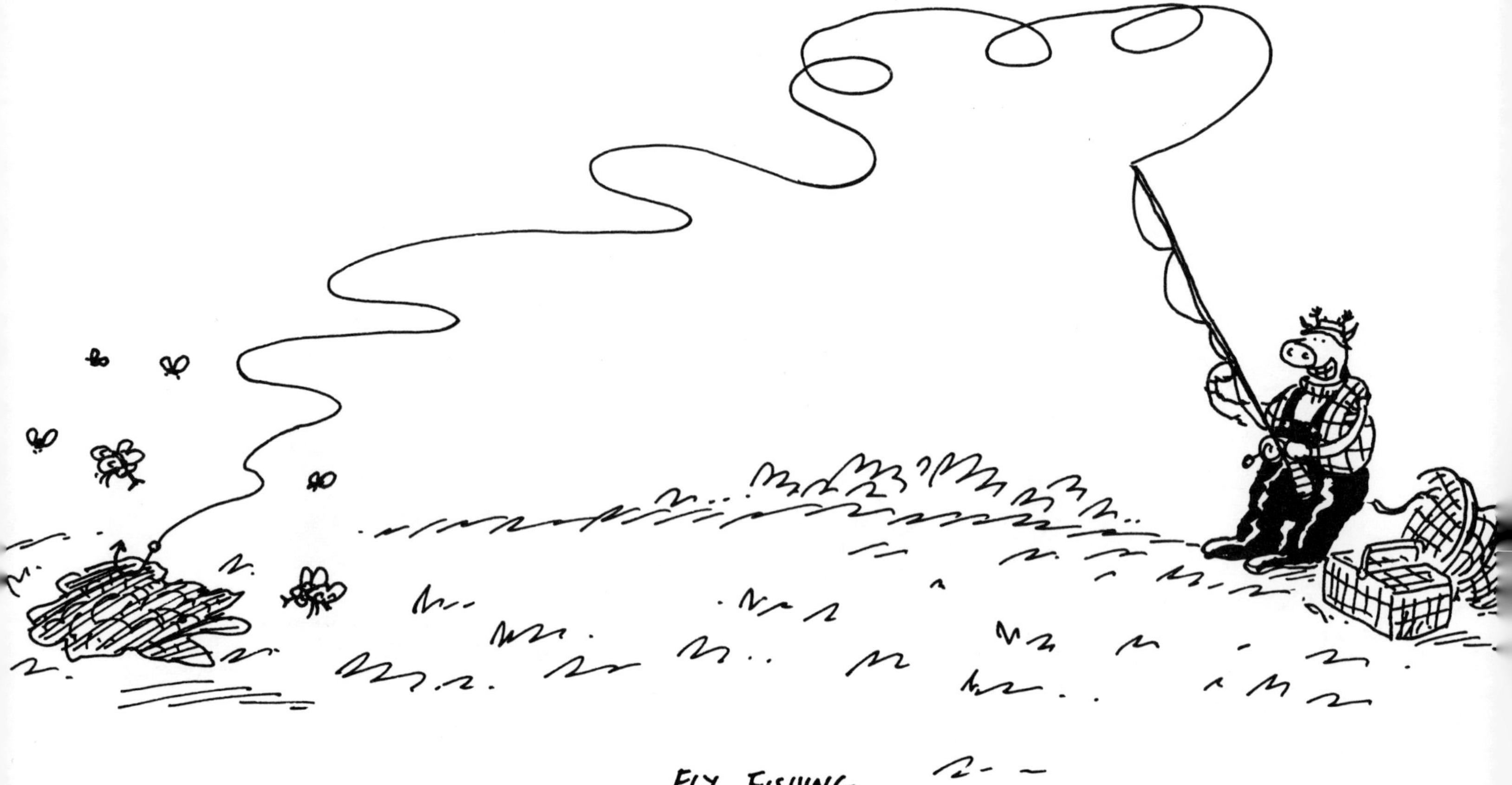

FLY FISHING

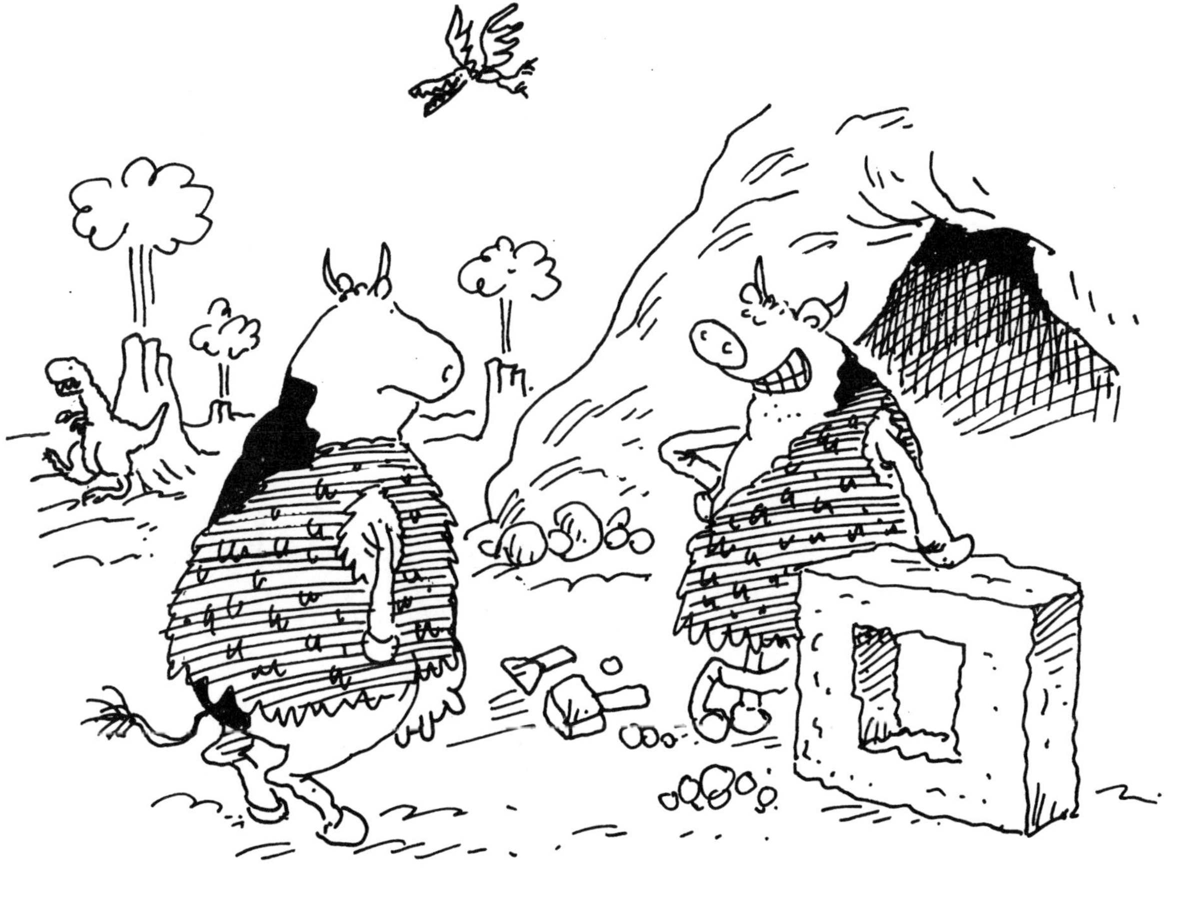

PLUNK!

MAD COW SHOT

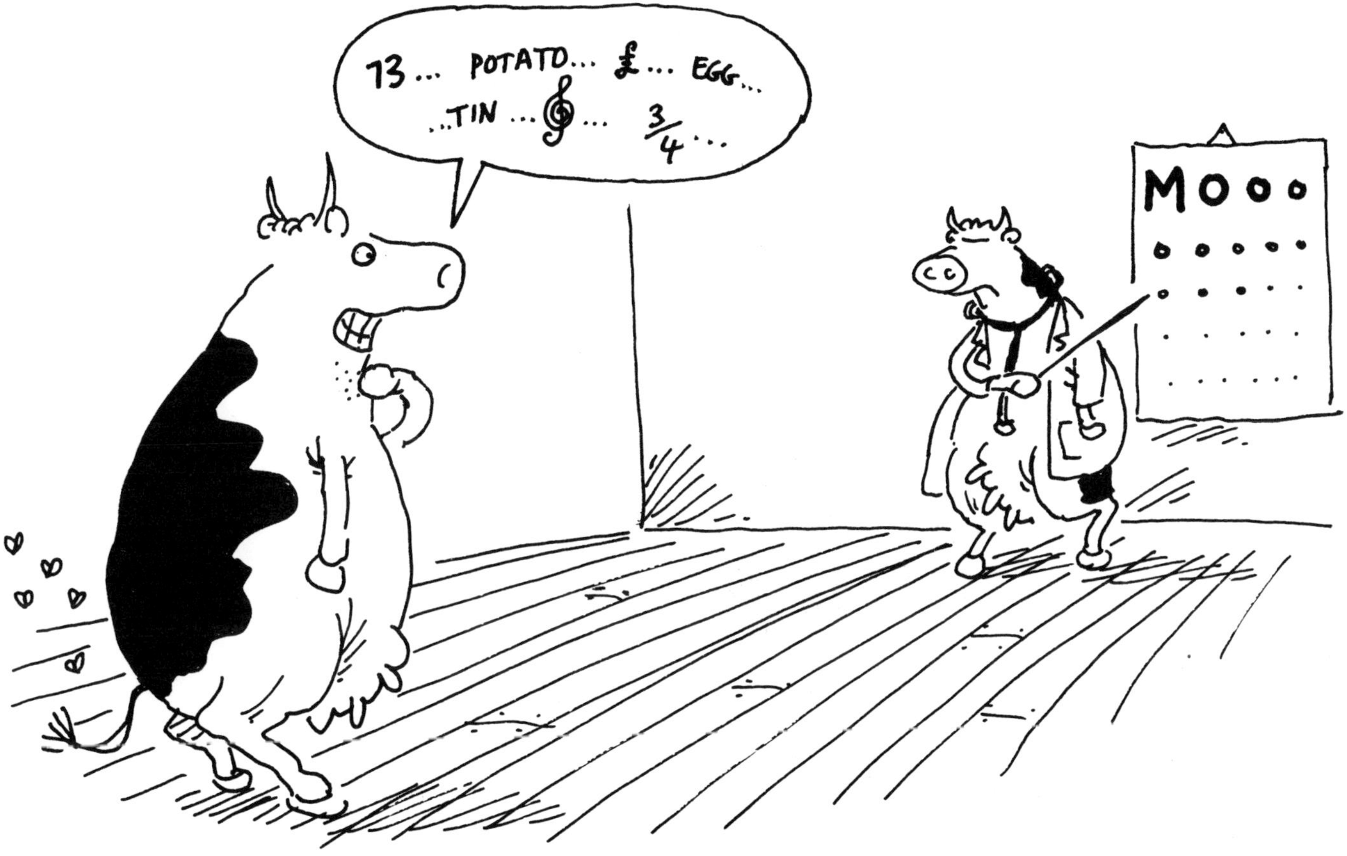
73... POTATO... £... EGG...
...TIN ... 𝄞 ... 3/4 ...
MOoo

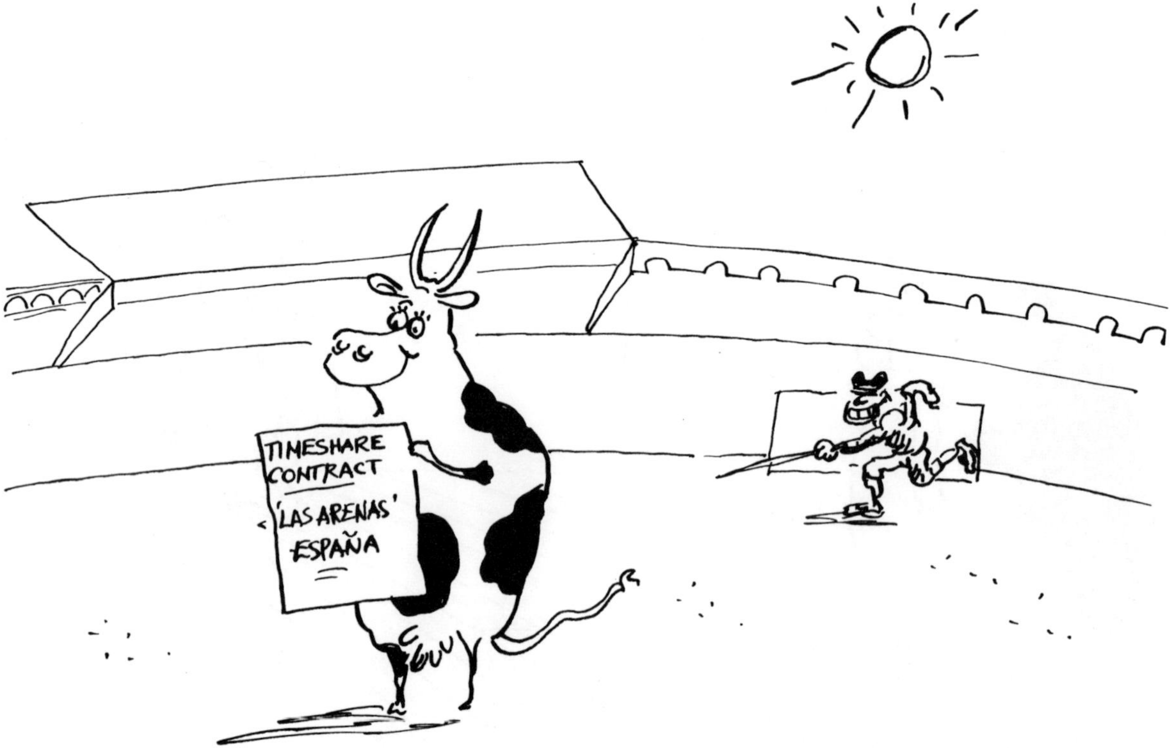
TIMESHARE
CONTRACT
'LAS ARENAS'
ESPAÑA

HOPPING MAD

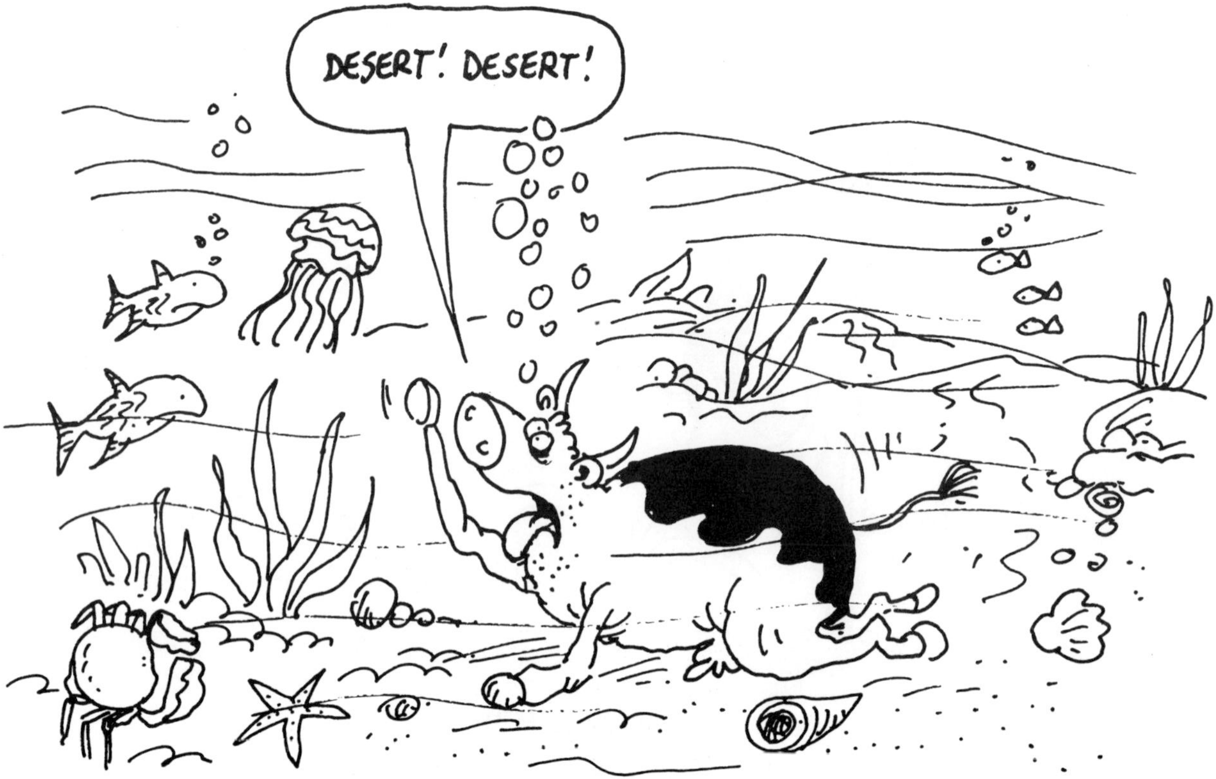
DESERT! DESERT!

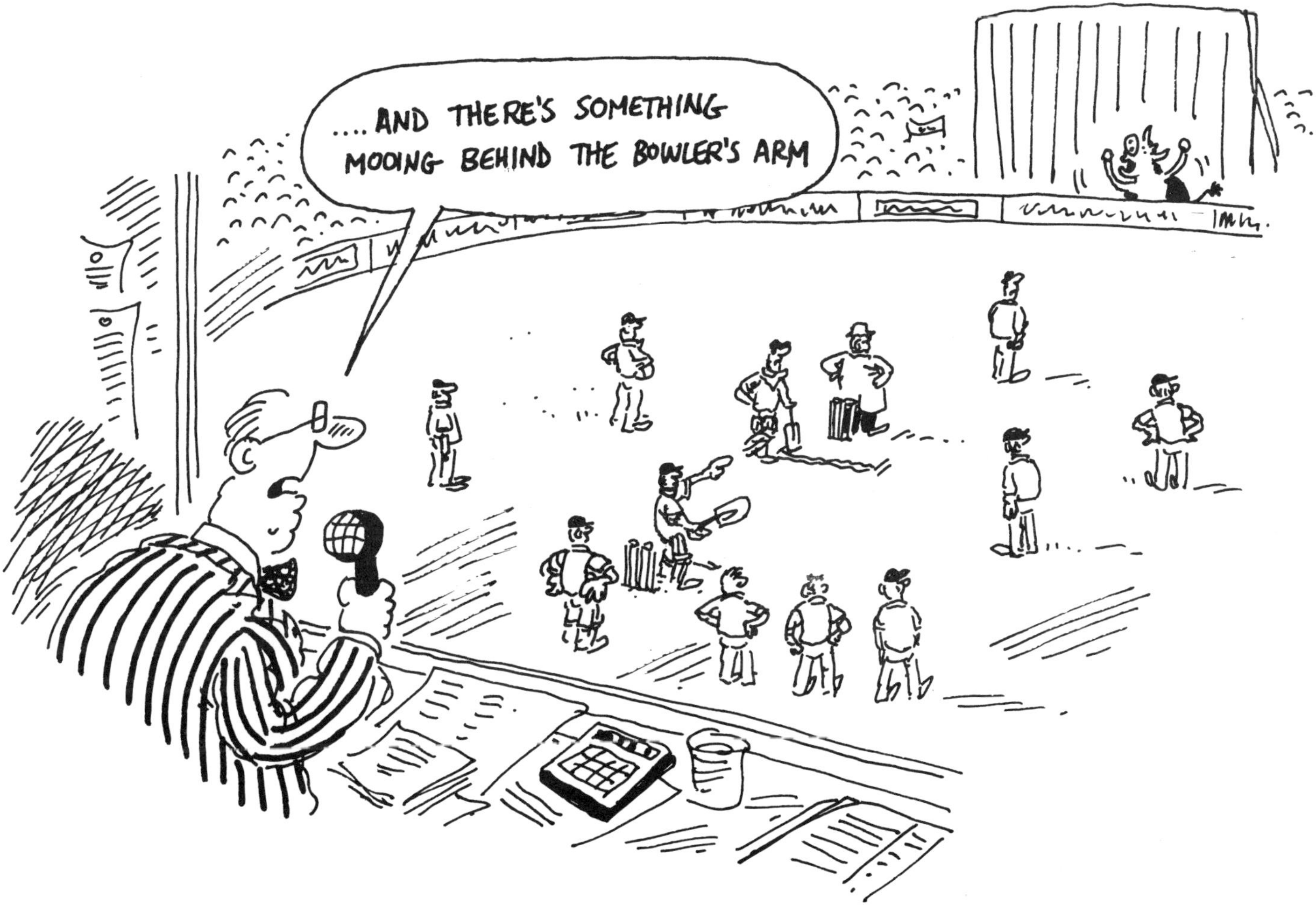
....AND THERE'S SOMETHING MOOING BEHIND THE BOWLER'S ARM

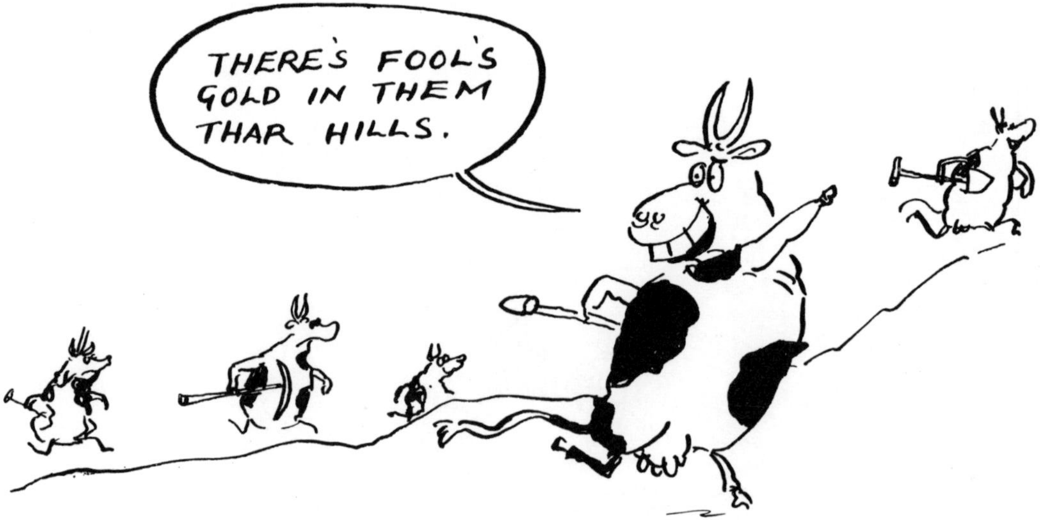
THERE'S FOOL'S GOLD IN THEM THAR HILLS.

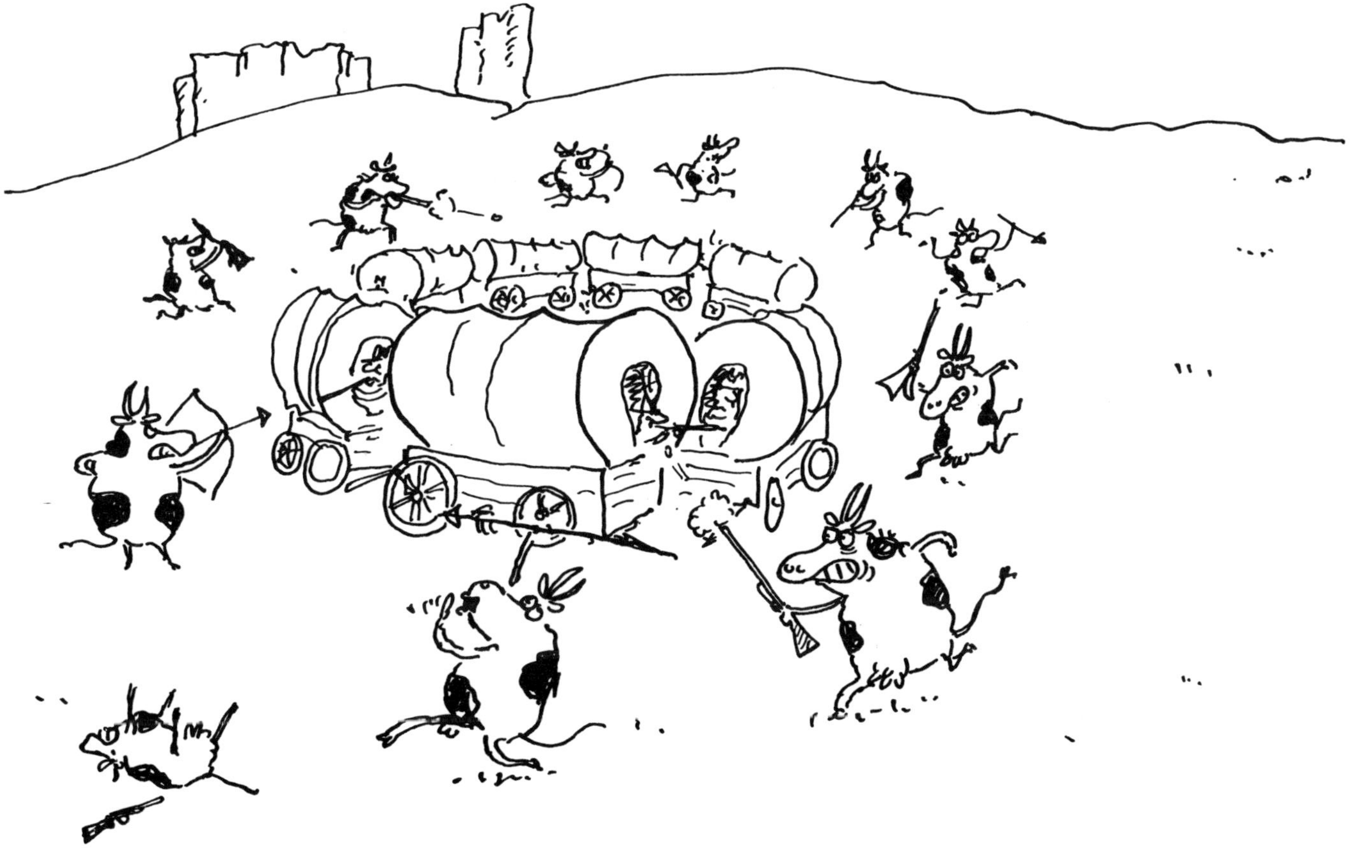

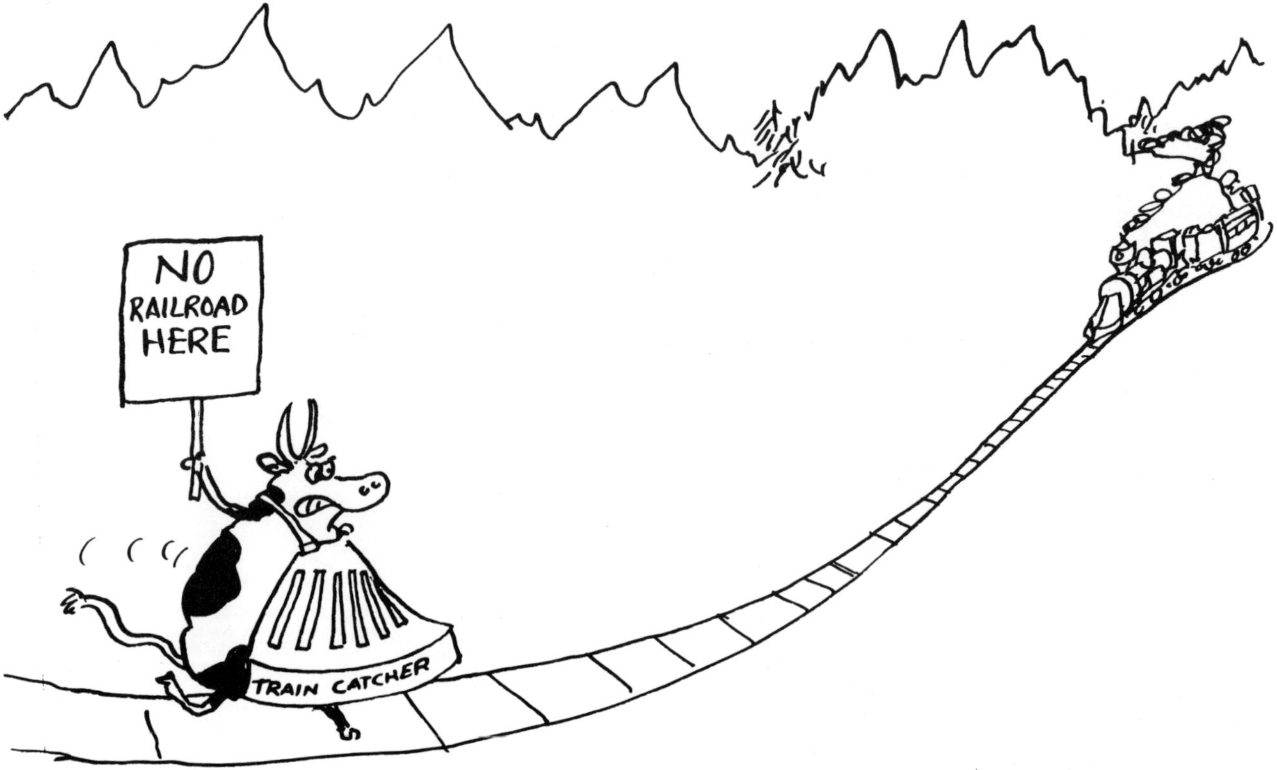
NO RAILROAD HERE
TRAIN CATCHER

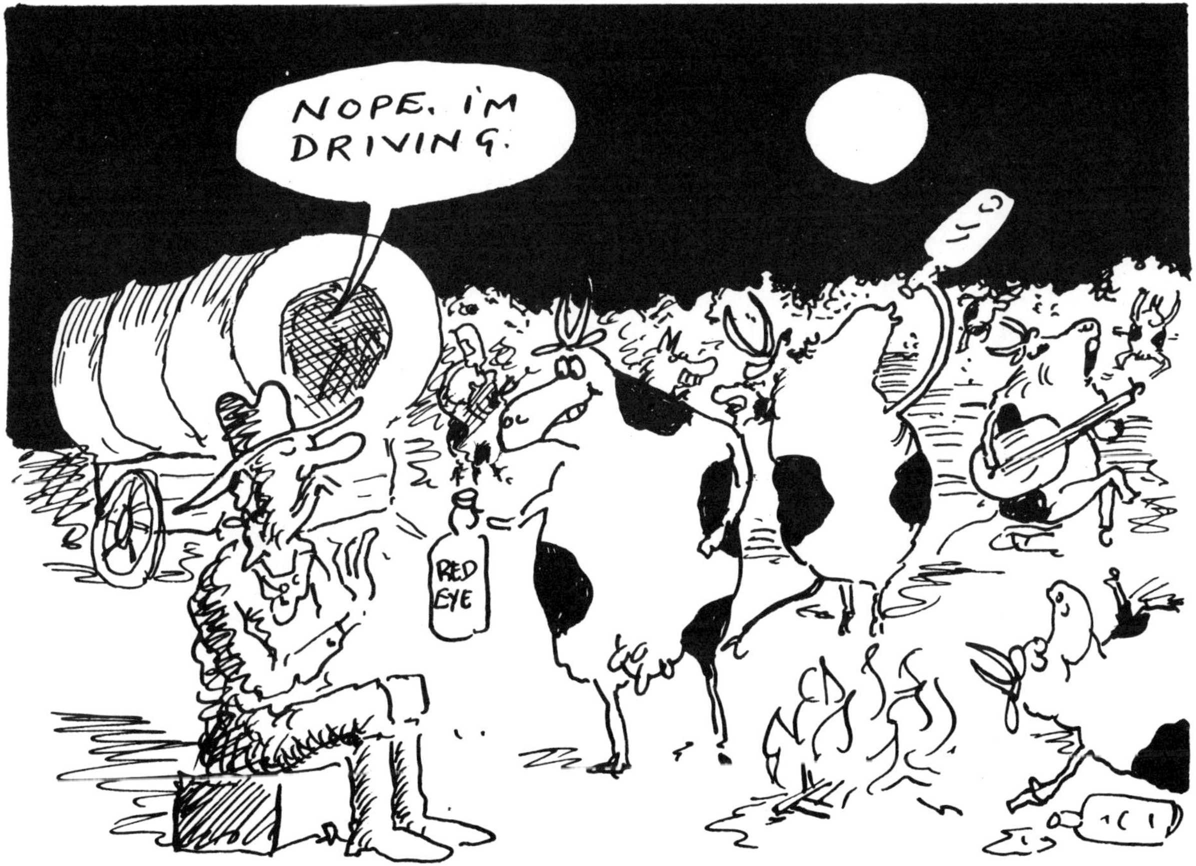
NOPE. I'M DRIVING.
RED EYE

AT NIGHT, NEARLY EVERYONE RELAXED ROUND THE CAMP FIRE.

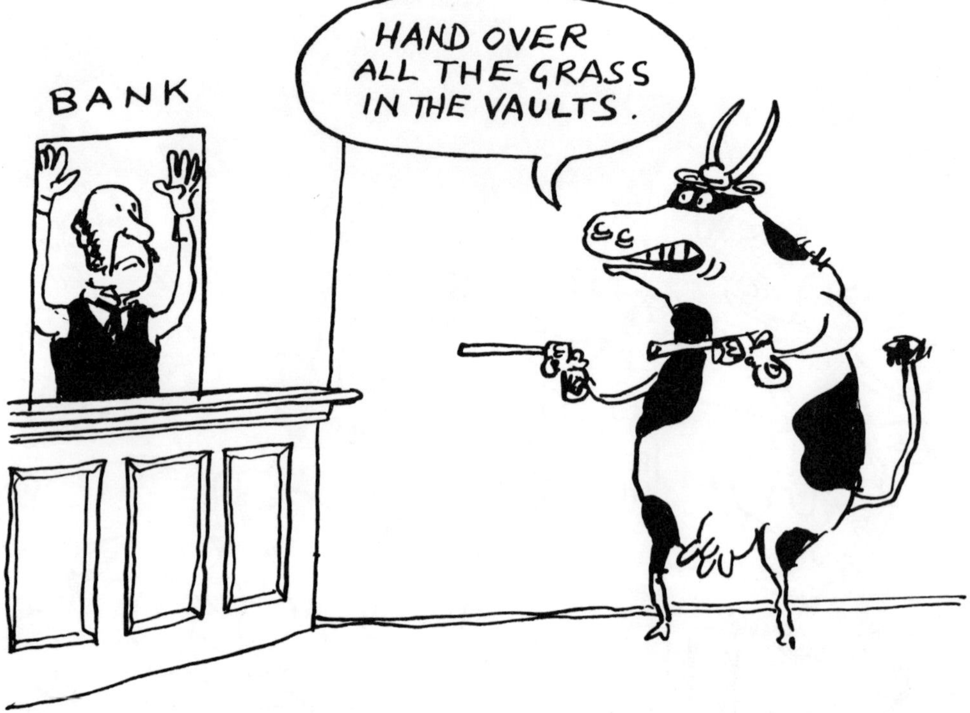
BANK
HAND OVER ALL THE GRASS IN THE VAULTS.

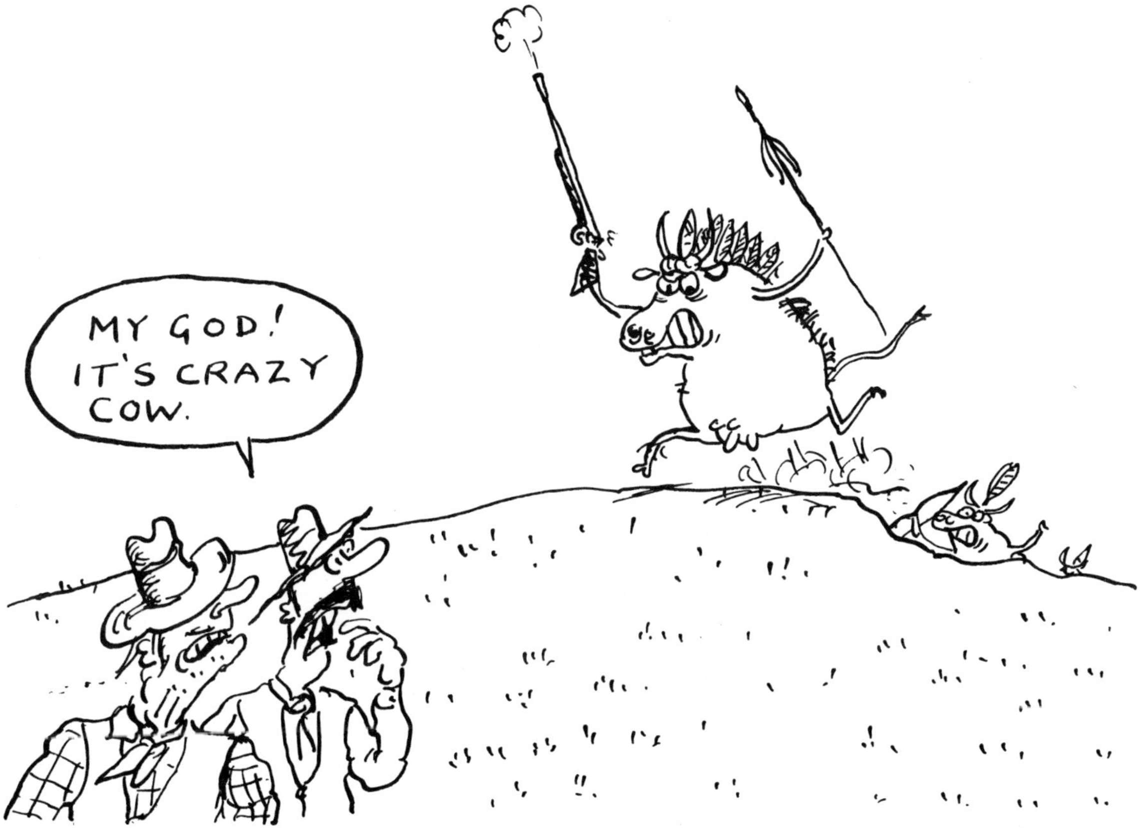
MY GOD! IT'S CRAZY COW.

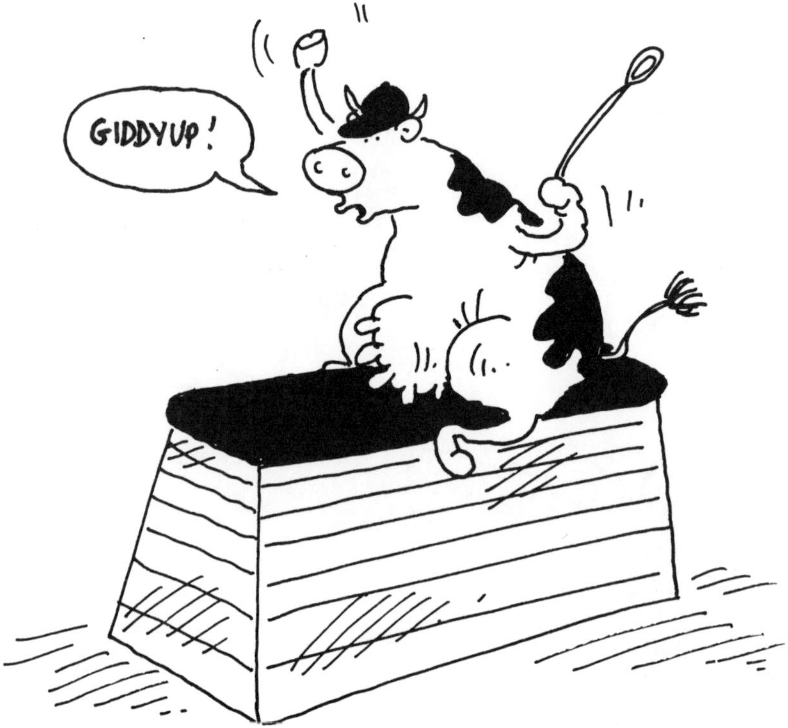
GIDDYUP!

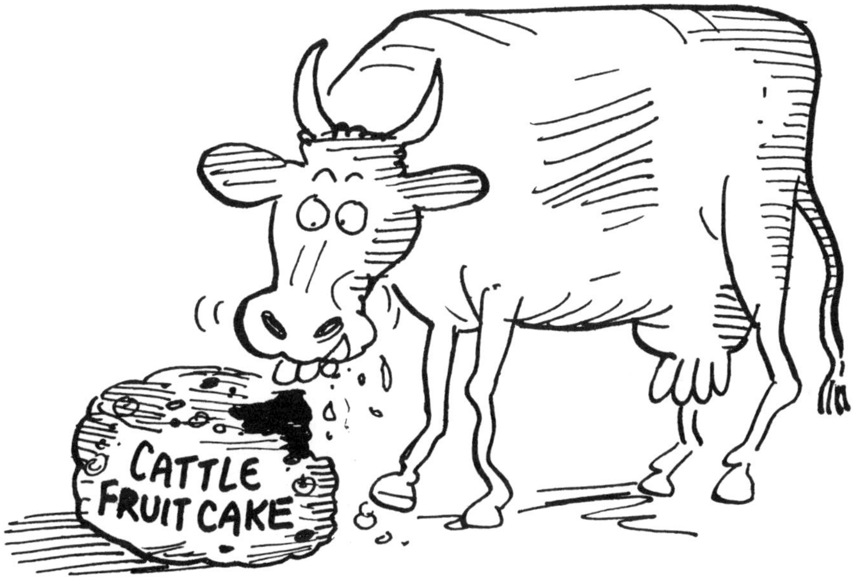
CATTLE
FRUIT CAKE

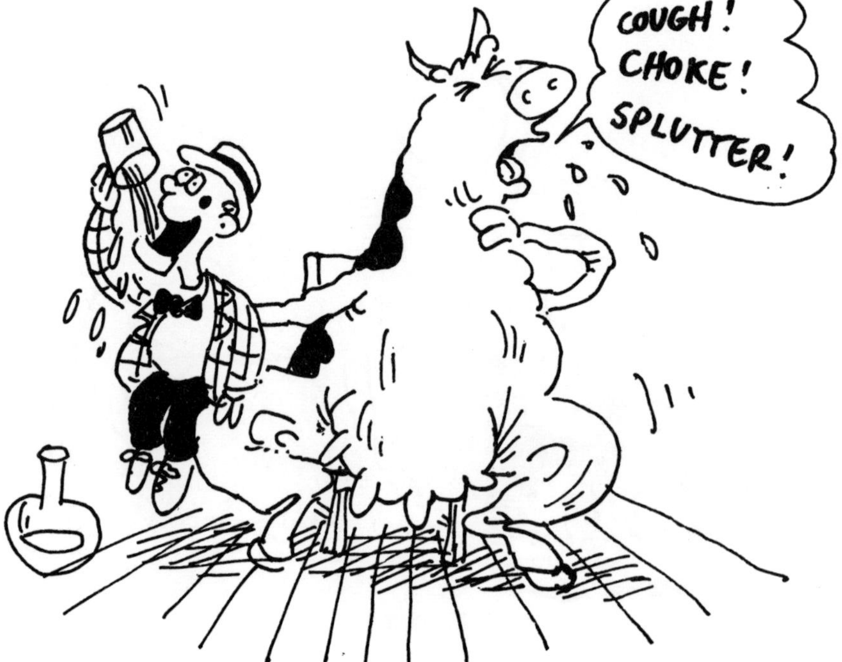
COUGH! CHOKE! SPLUTTER!

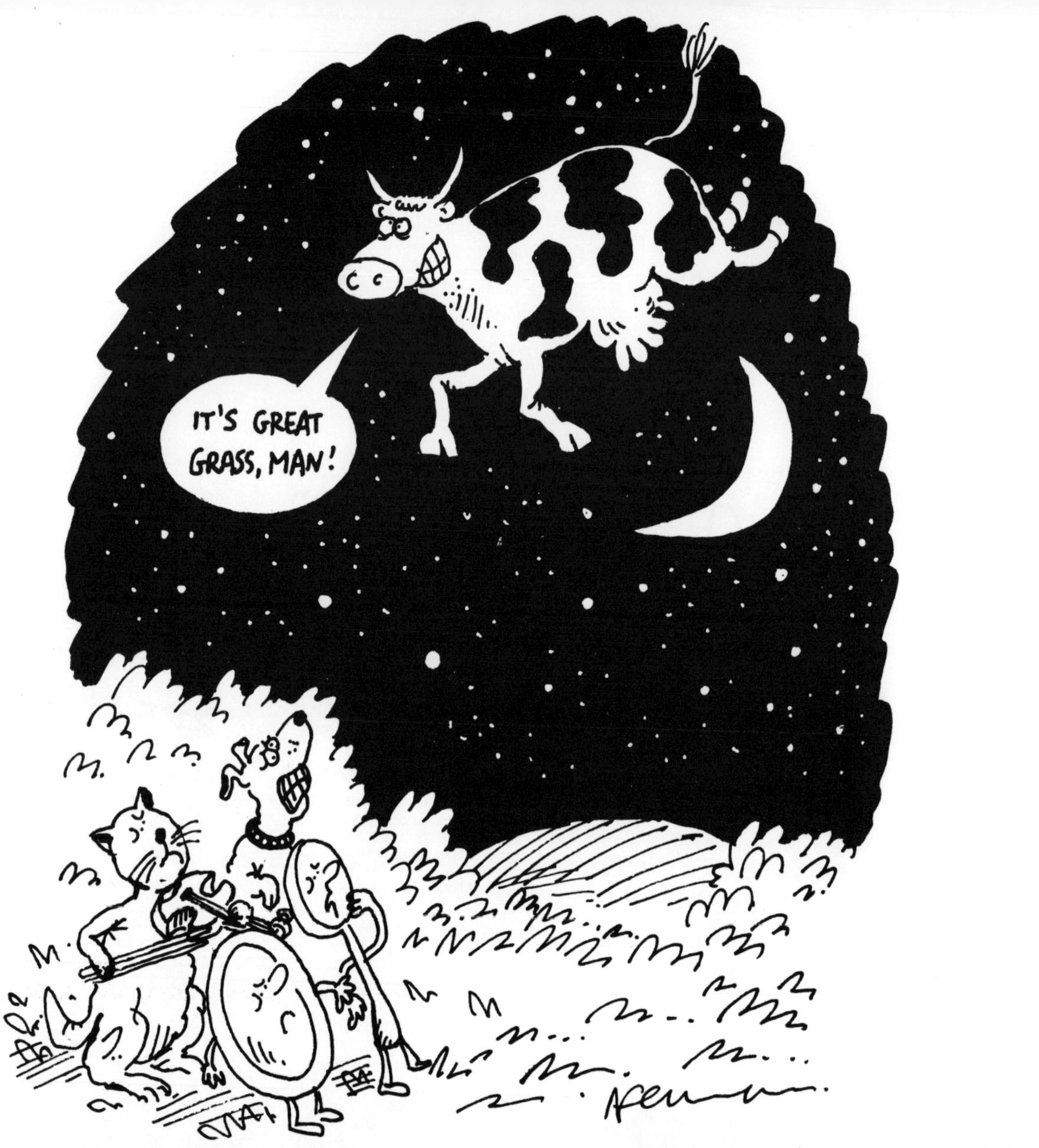
IT'S GREAT GRASS, MAN!

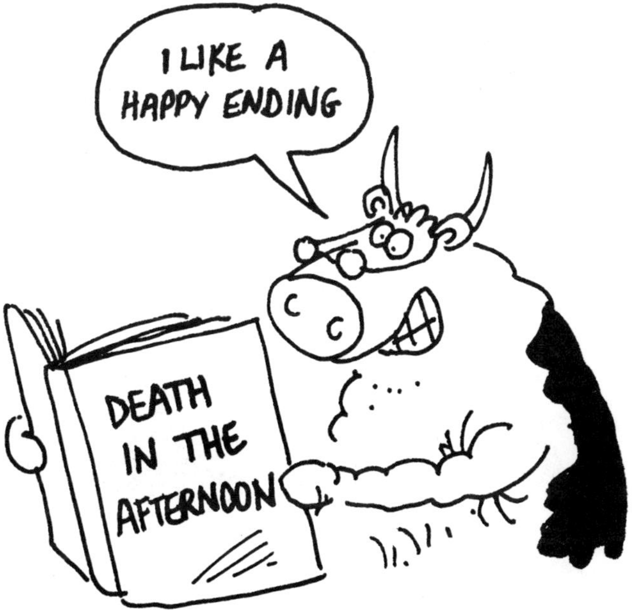
I LIKE A HAPPY ENDING
DEATH IN THE AFTERNOON

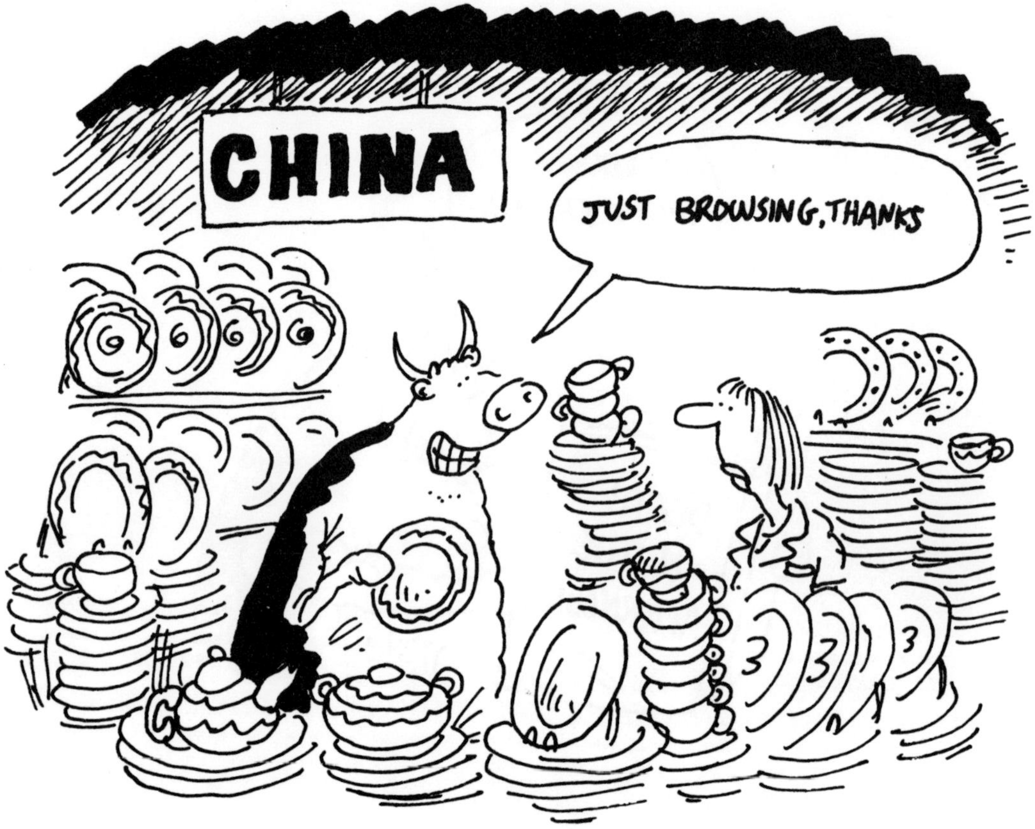
CHINA
JUST BROWSING, THANKS

CAT STEVENS
GREATEST HITS
BRISKET DONOR CARD

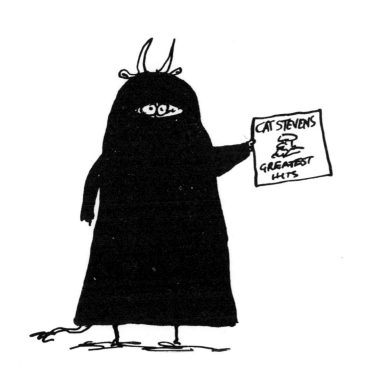

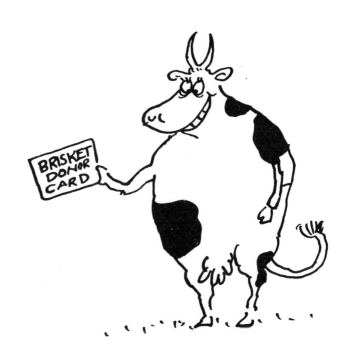

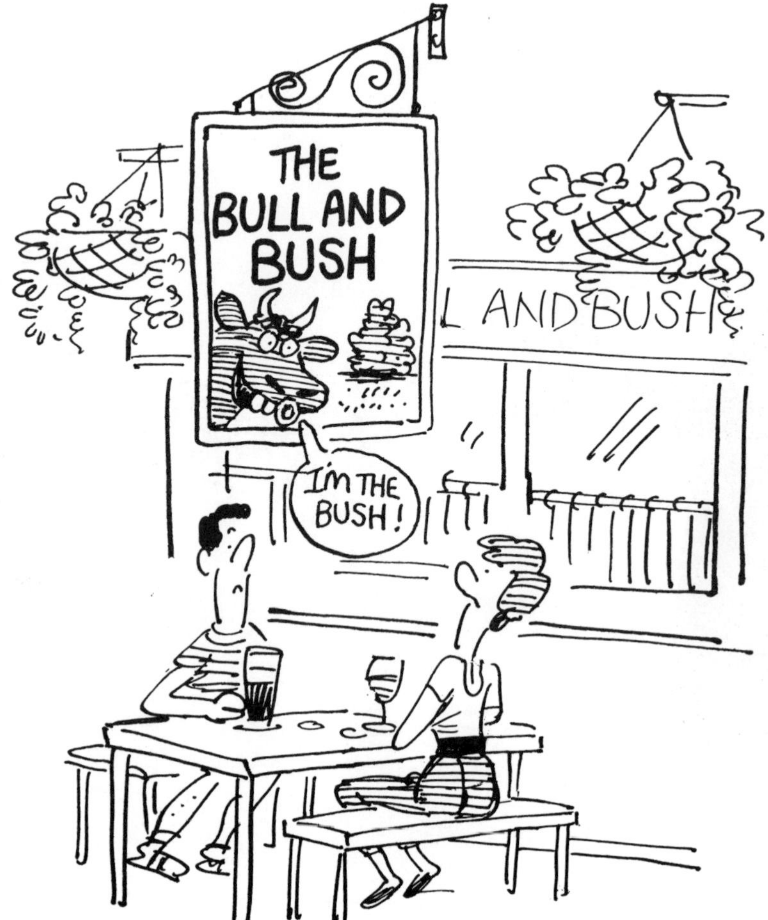
THE BULL AND BUSH
L AND BUSH
I'M THE BUSH!

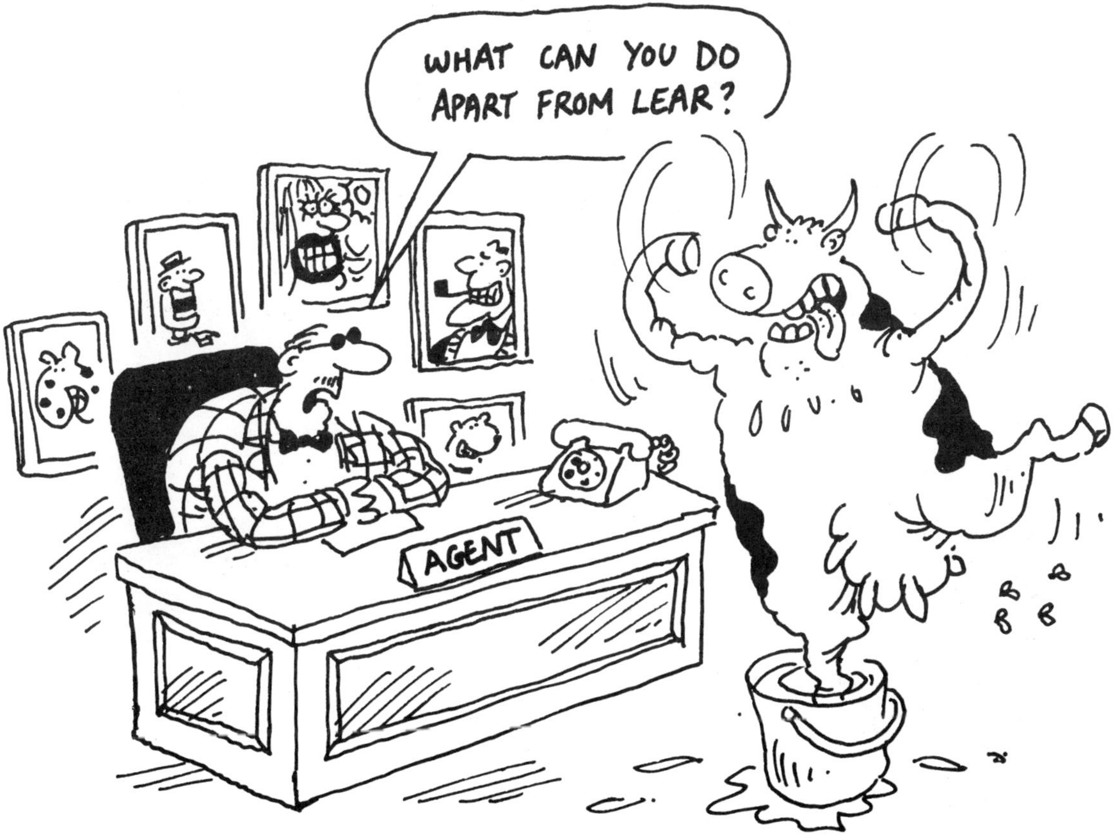
WHAT CAN YOU DO APART FROM LEAR?
AGENT

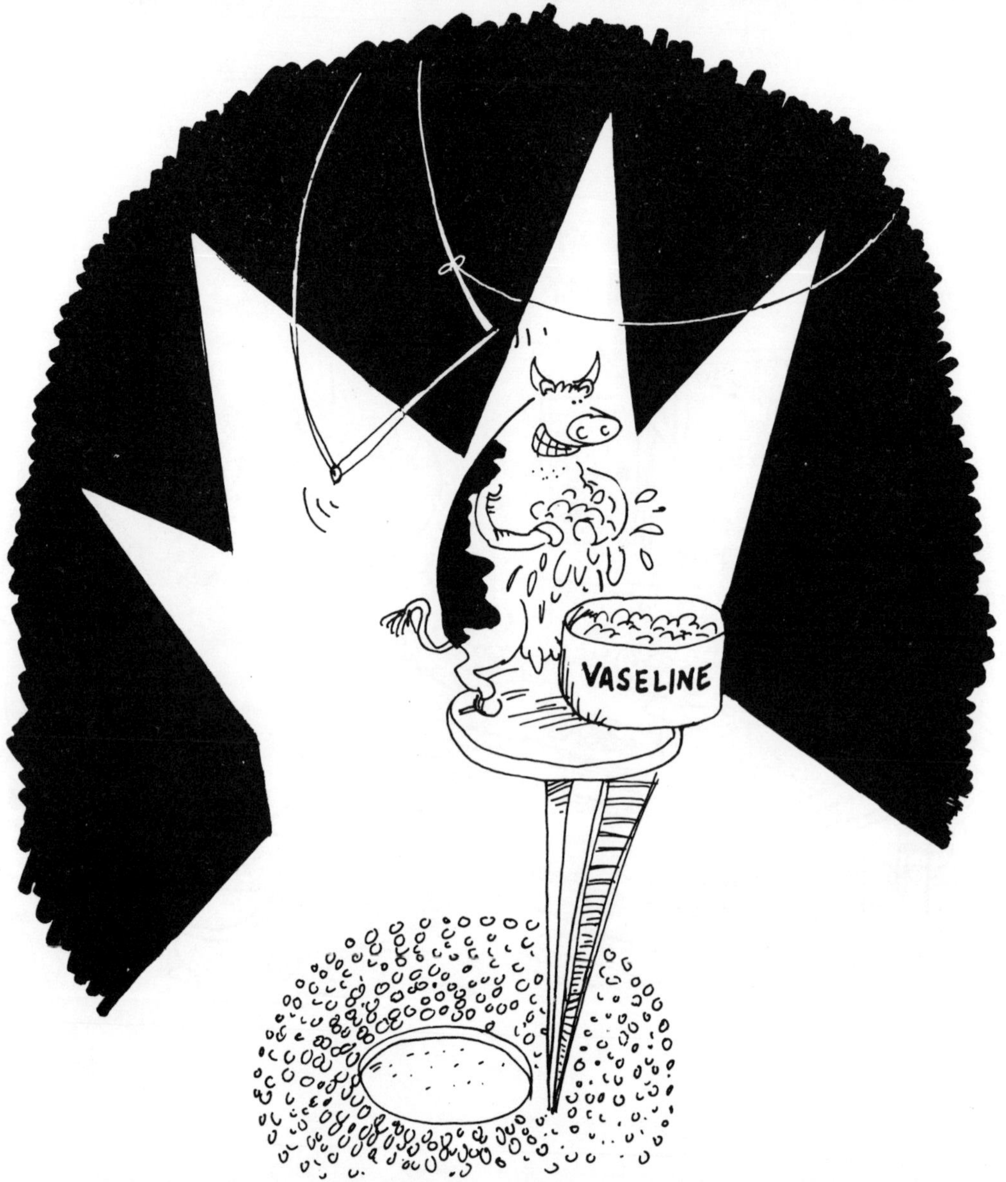
VASELINE

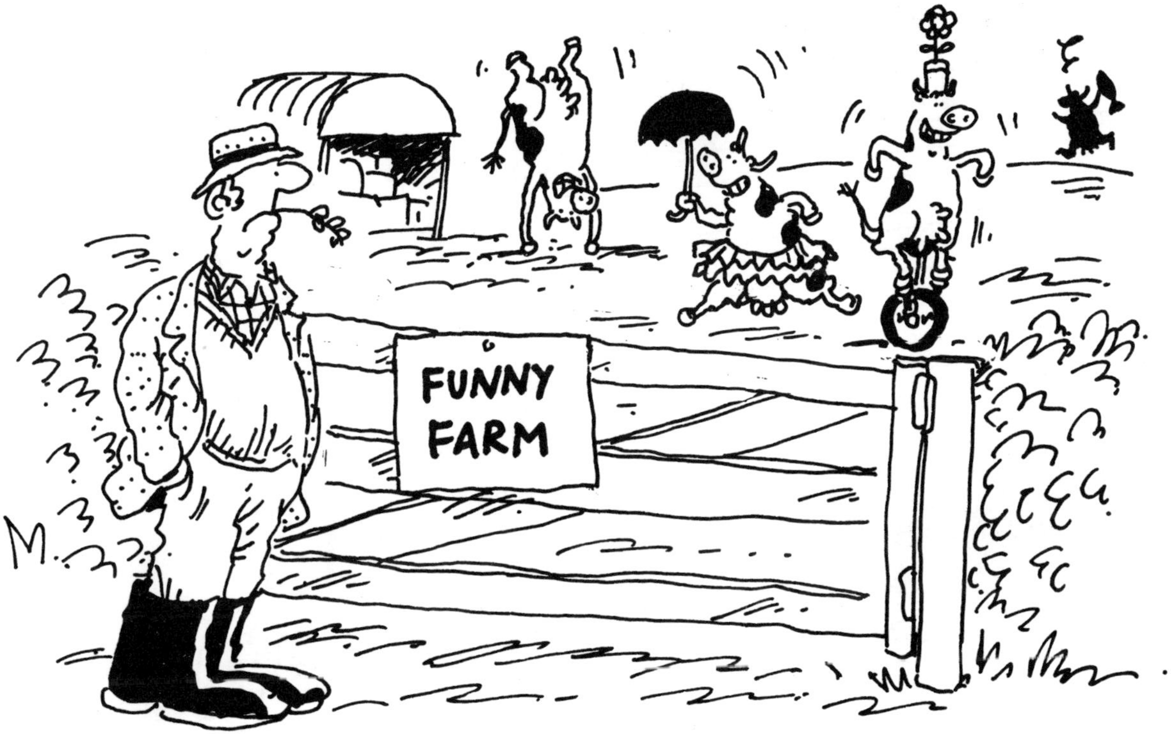
FUNNY
FARM

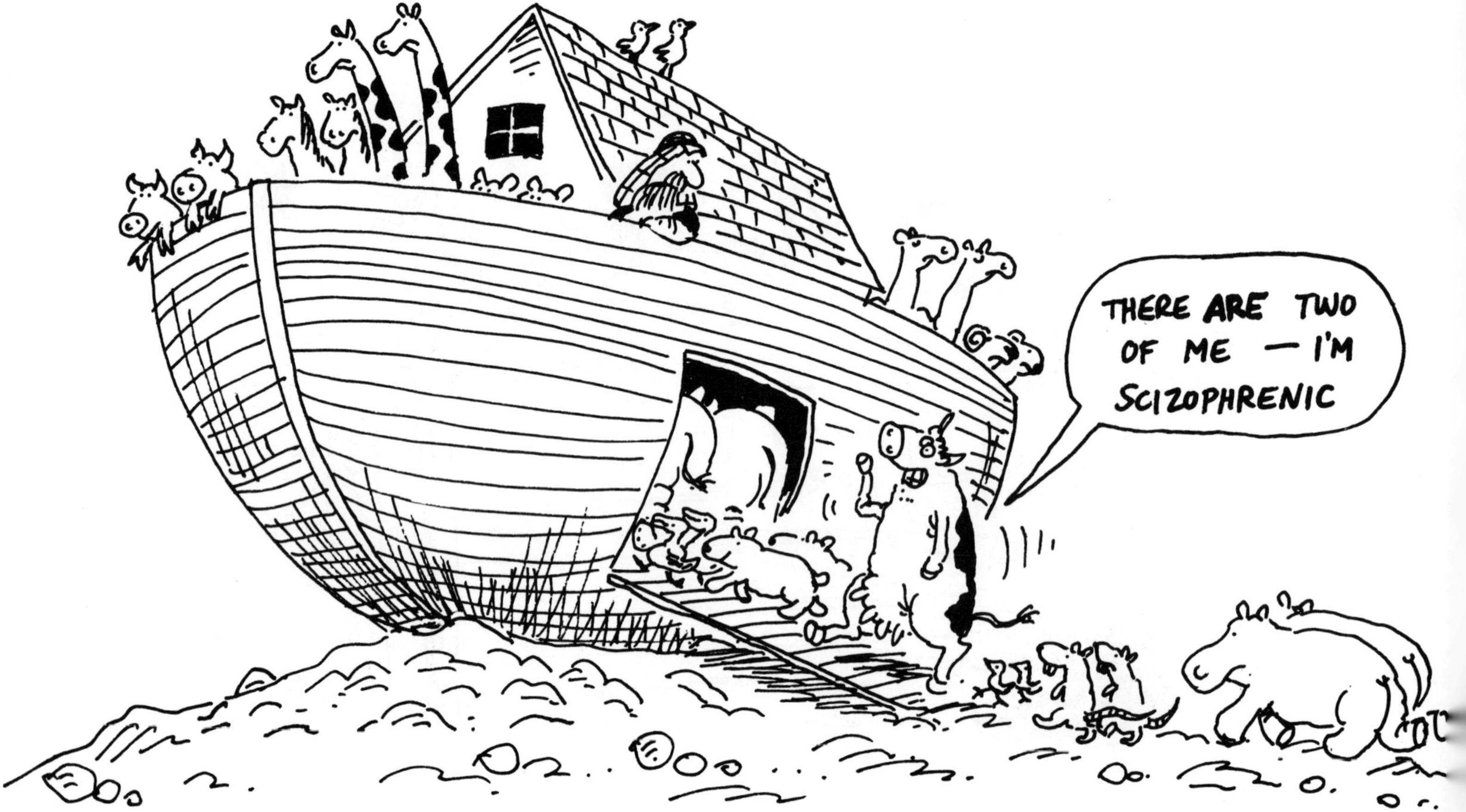
THERE ARE TWO OF ME — I'M SCIZOPHRENIC

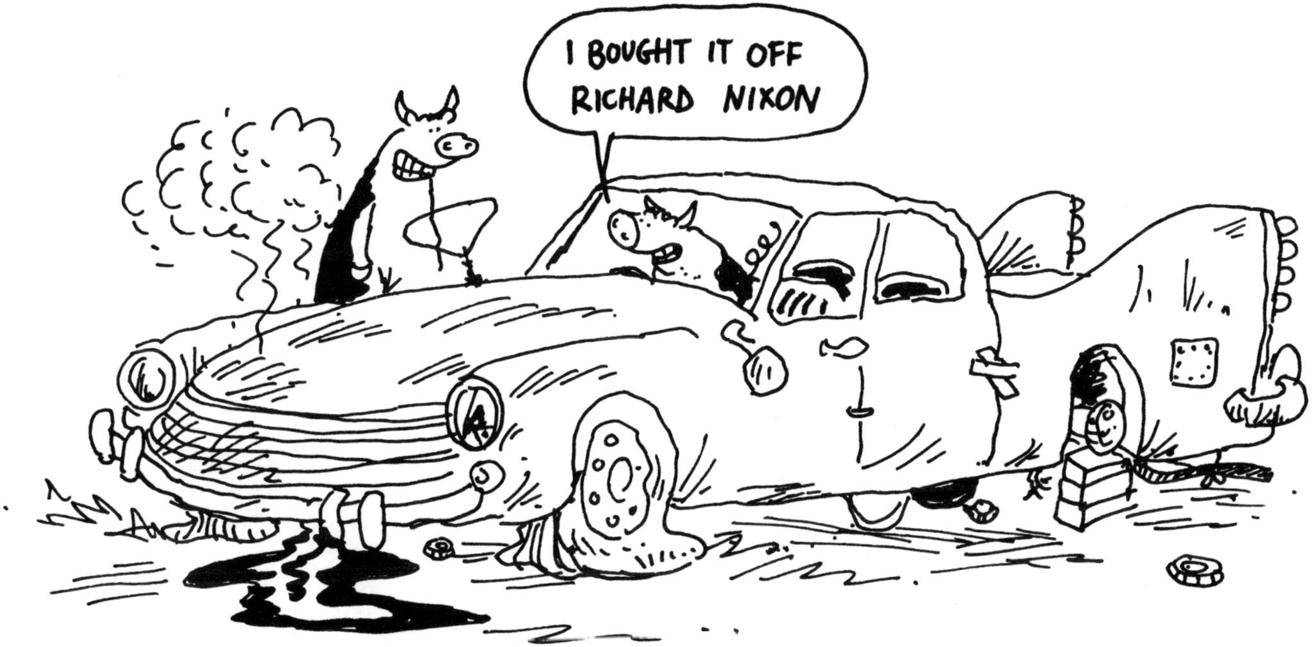
I BOUGHT IT OFF RICHARD NIXON

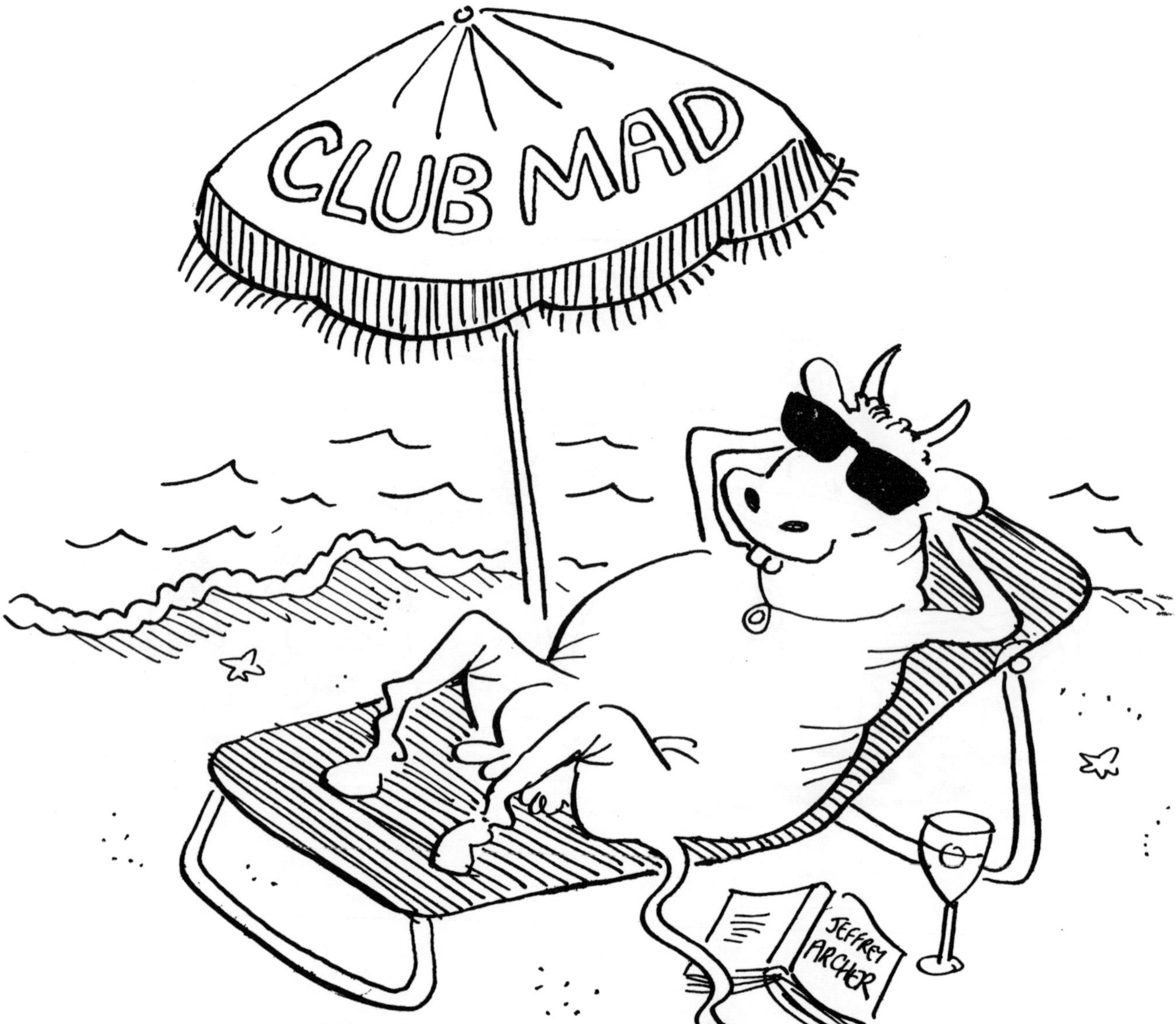
CLUB MAD
JEFFREY ARCHER

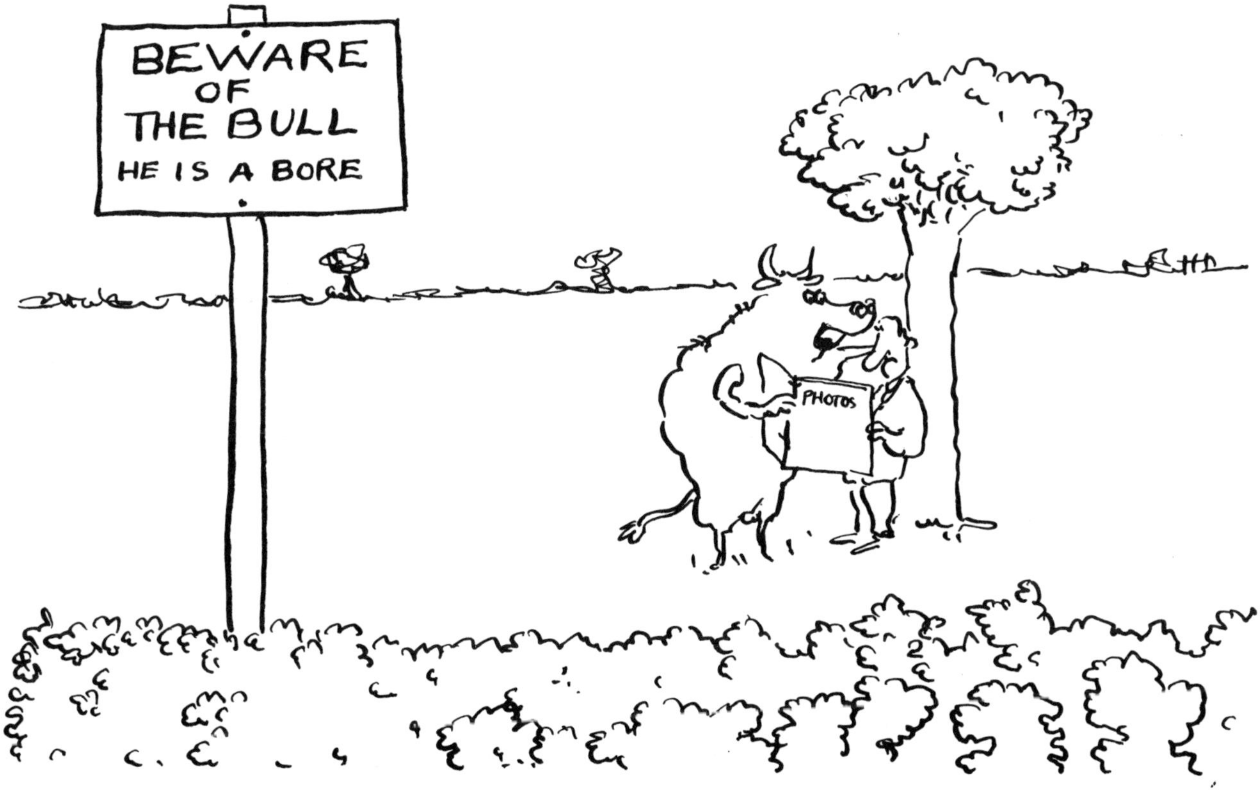
BEWARE
OF
THE BULL
HE IS A BORE
PHOTOS

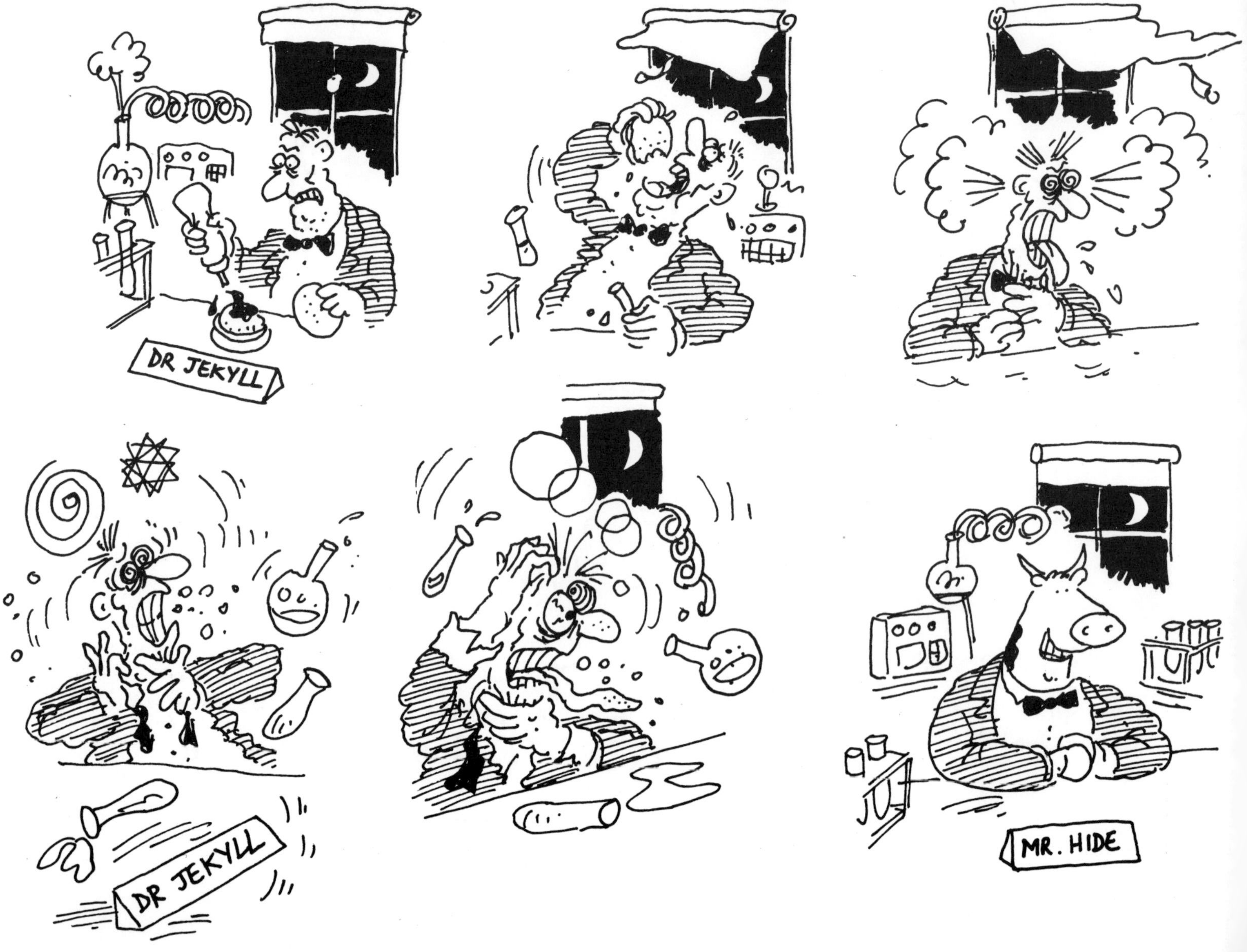
DR JEKYLL
DR JEKYLL
MR. HIDE

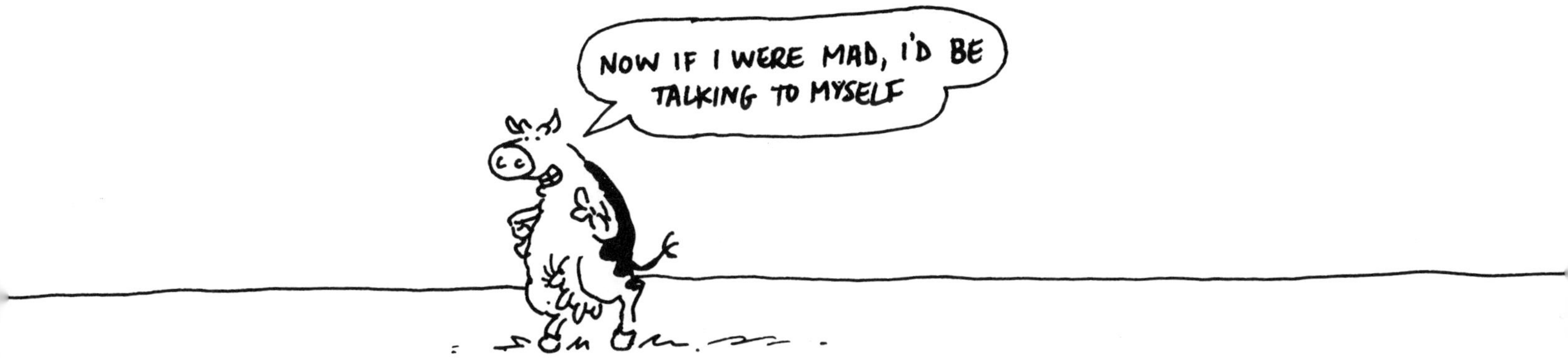
NOW IF I WERE MAD, I'D BE TALKING TO MYSELF

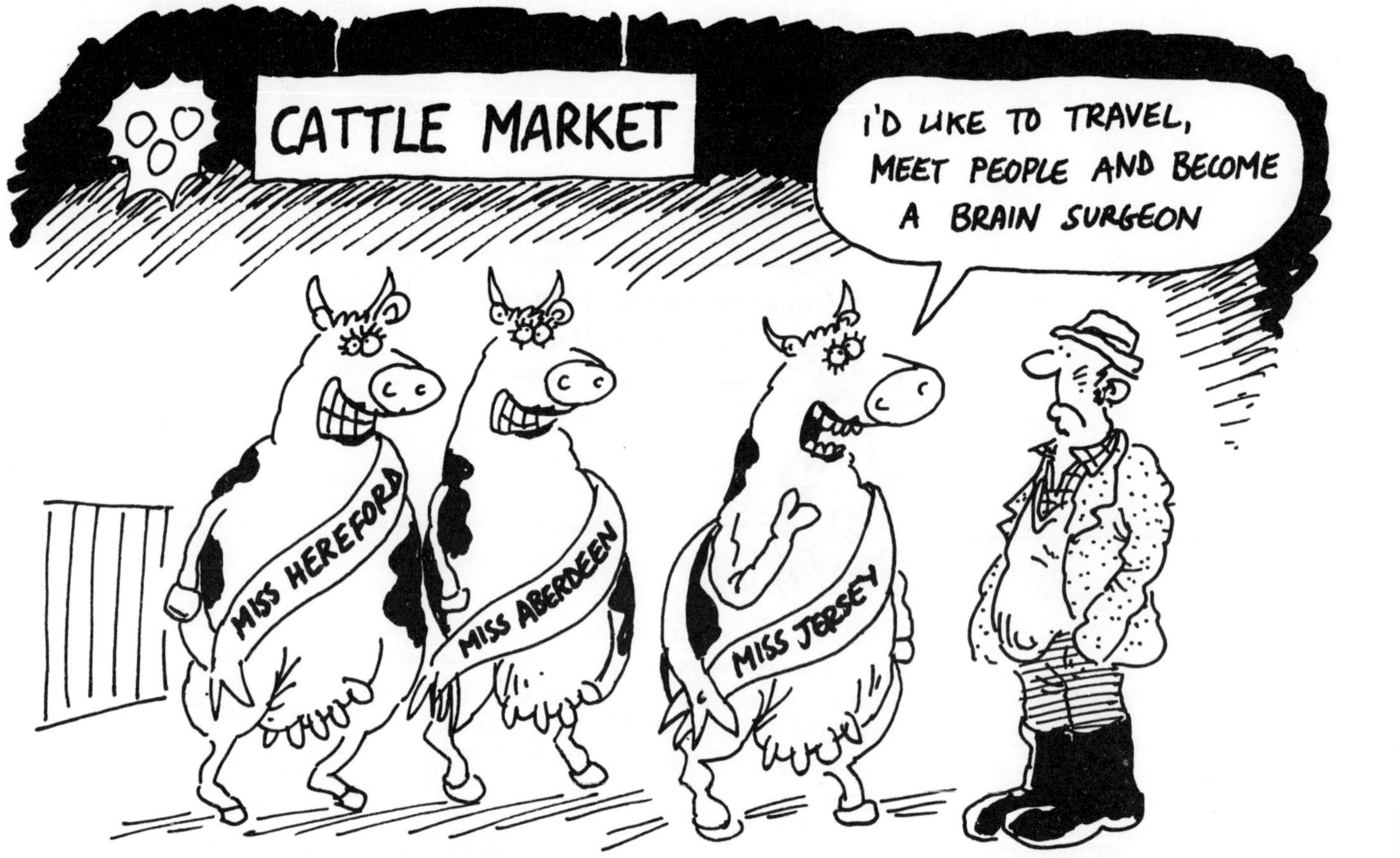
CATTLE MARKET
I'D LIKE TO TRAVEL, MEET PEOPLE AND BECOME A BRAIN SURGEON
MISS HEREFORD
MISS ABERDEEN
MISS JERSEY

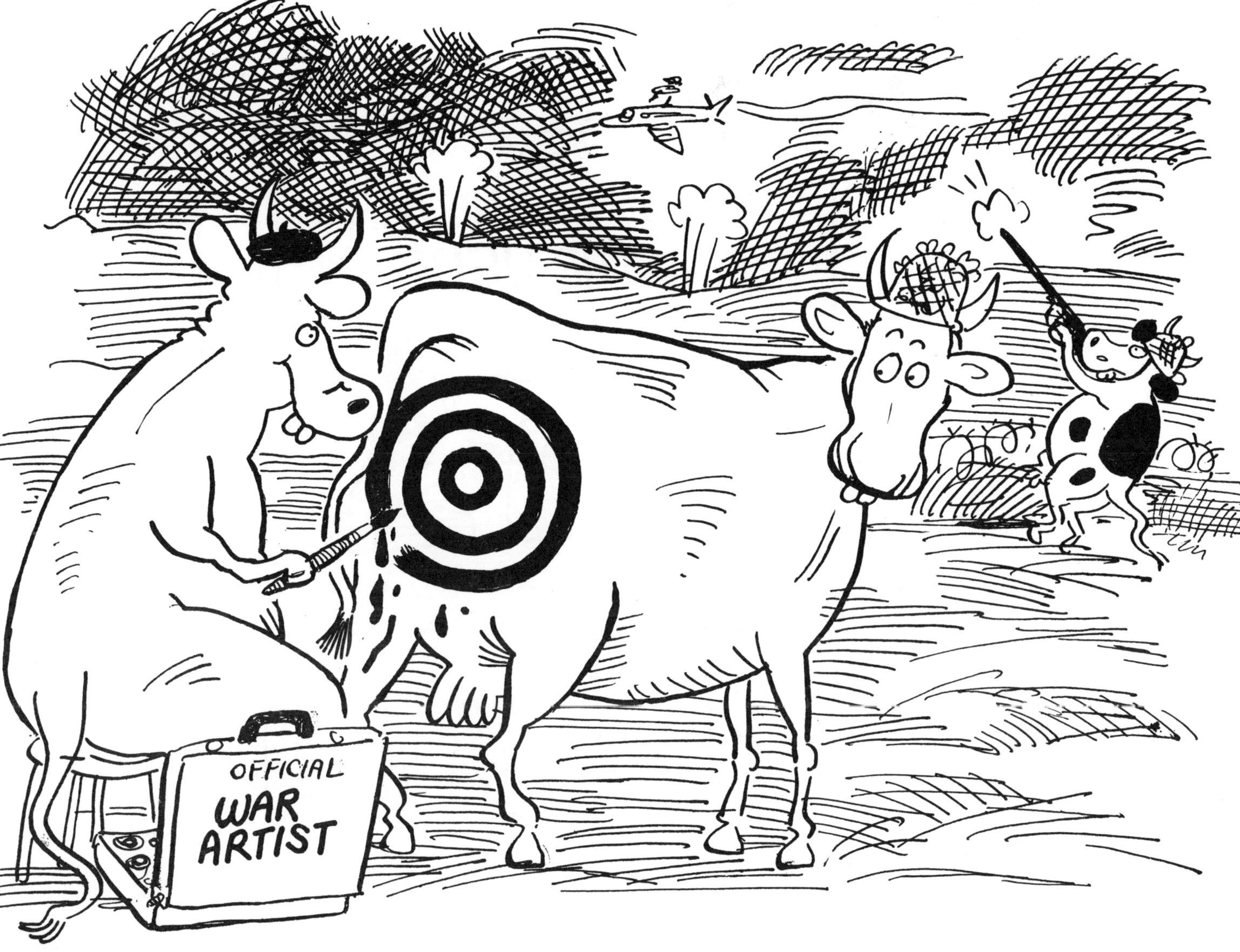
OFFICIAL
WAR
ARTIST

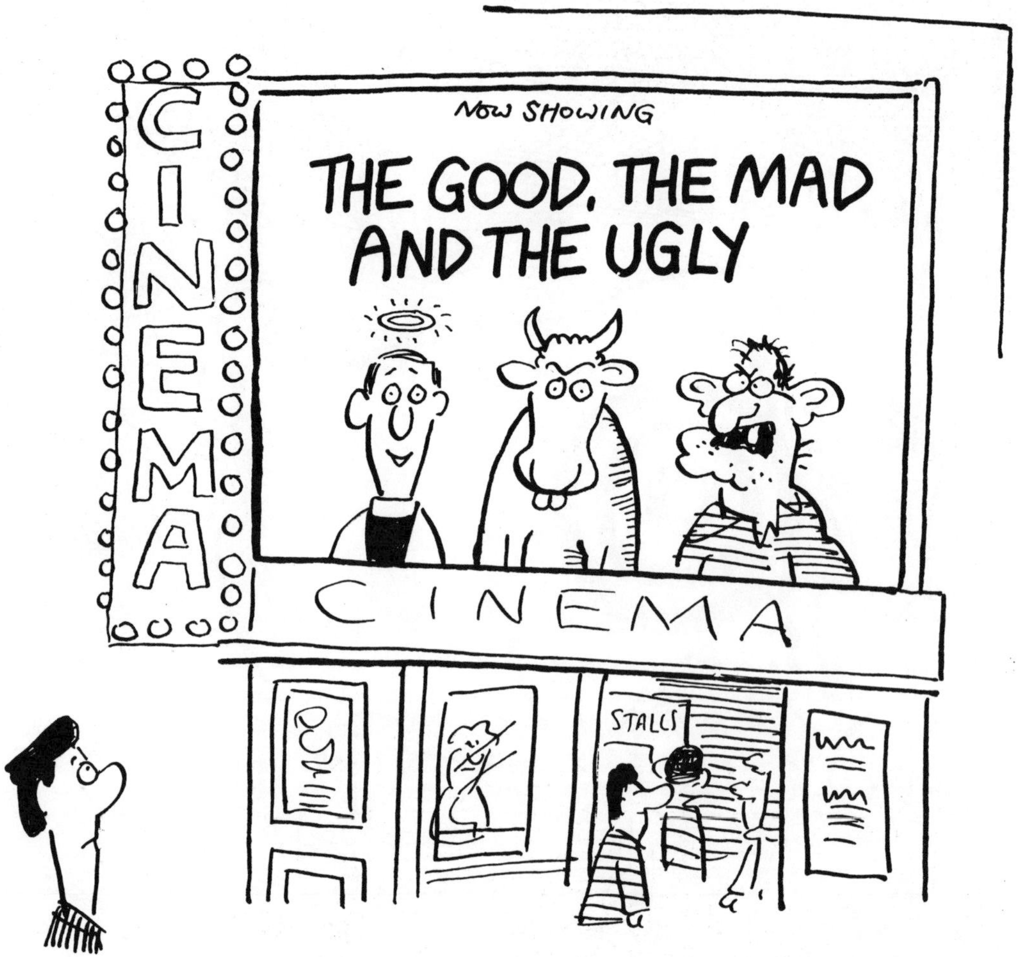
CINEMA
NOW SHOWING
THE GOOD, THE MAD AND THE UGLY
CINEMA
STALLS

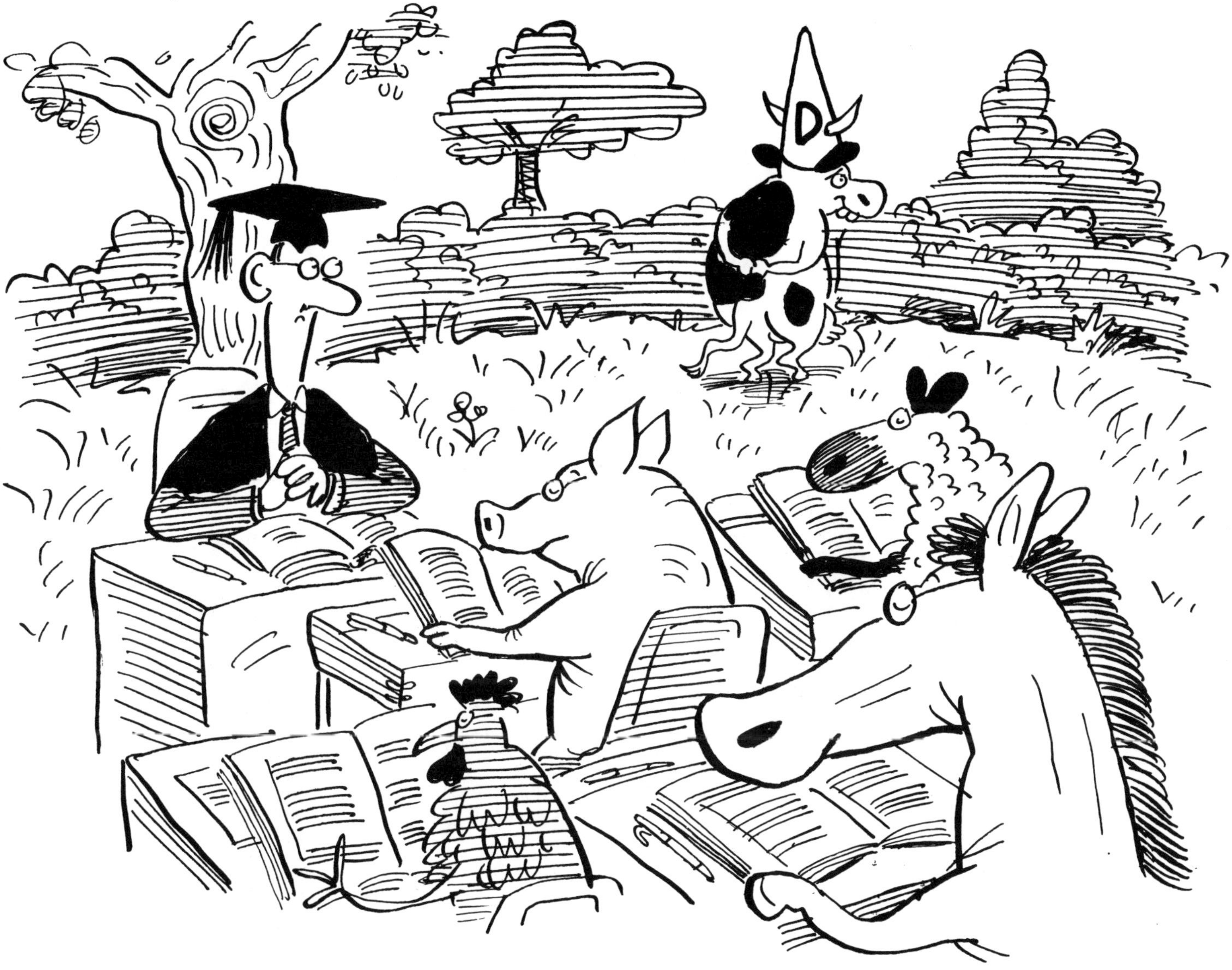

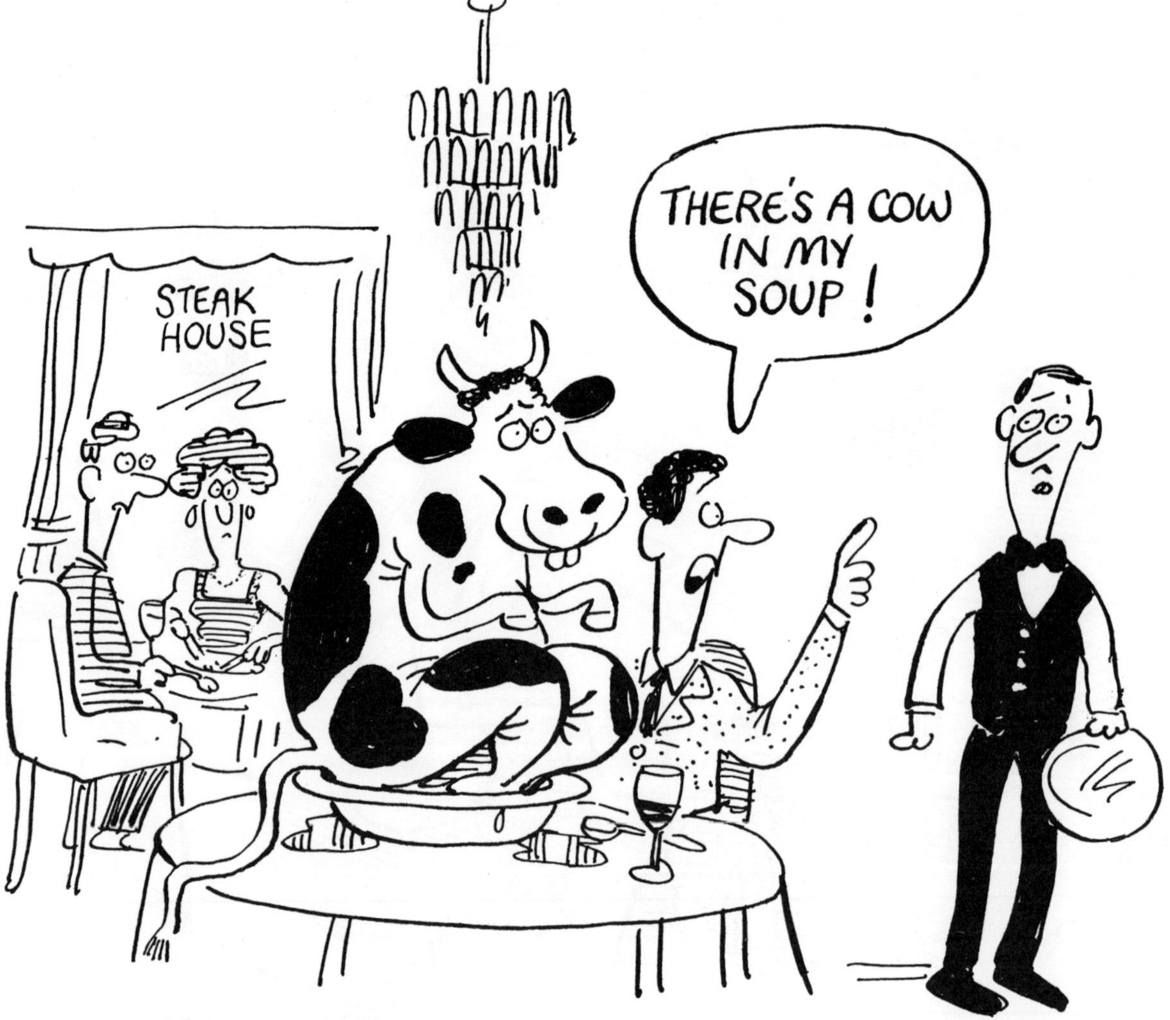
STEAK HOUSE
THERE'S A COW IN MY SOUP !

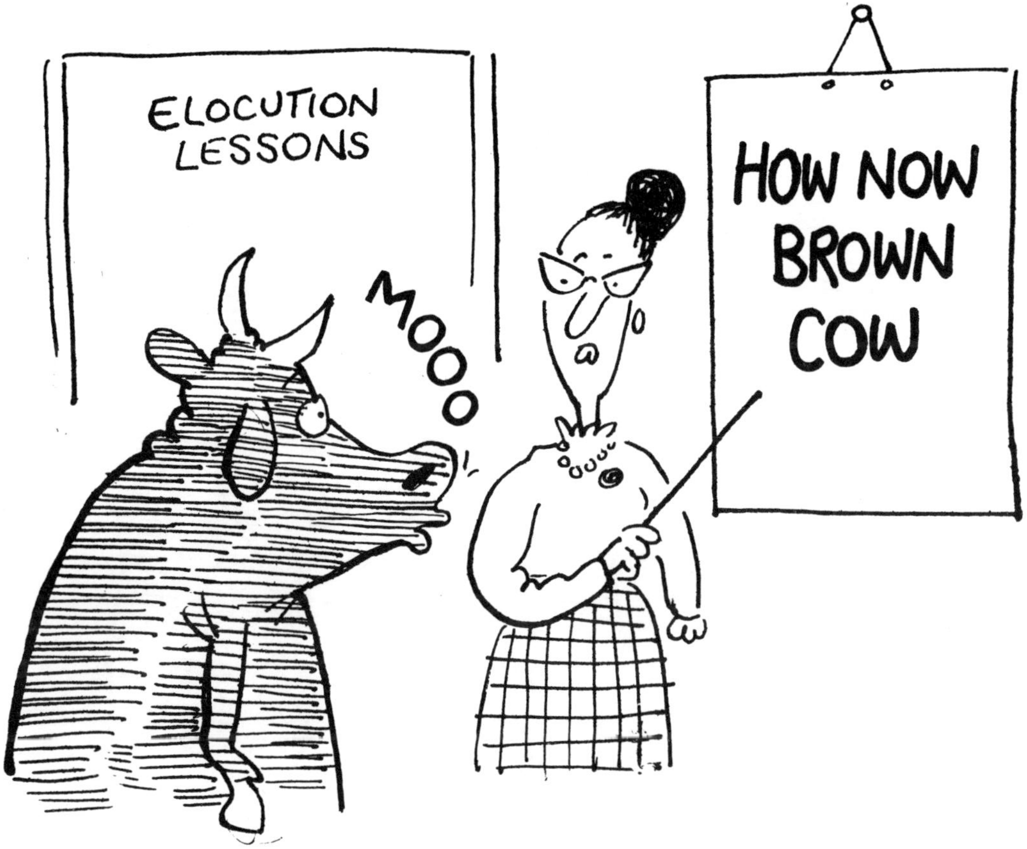
ELOCUTION LESSONS
MOOO
HOW NOW BROWN COW

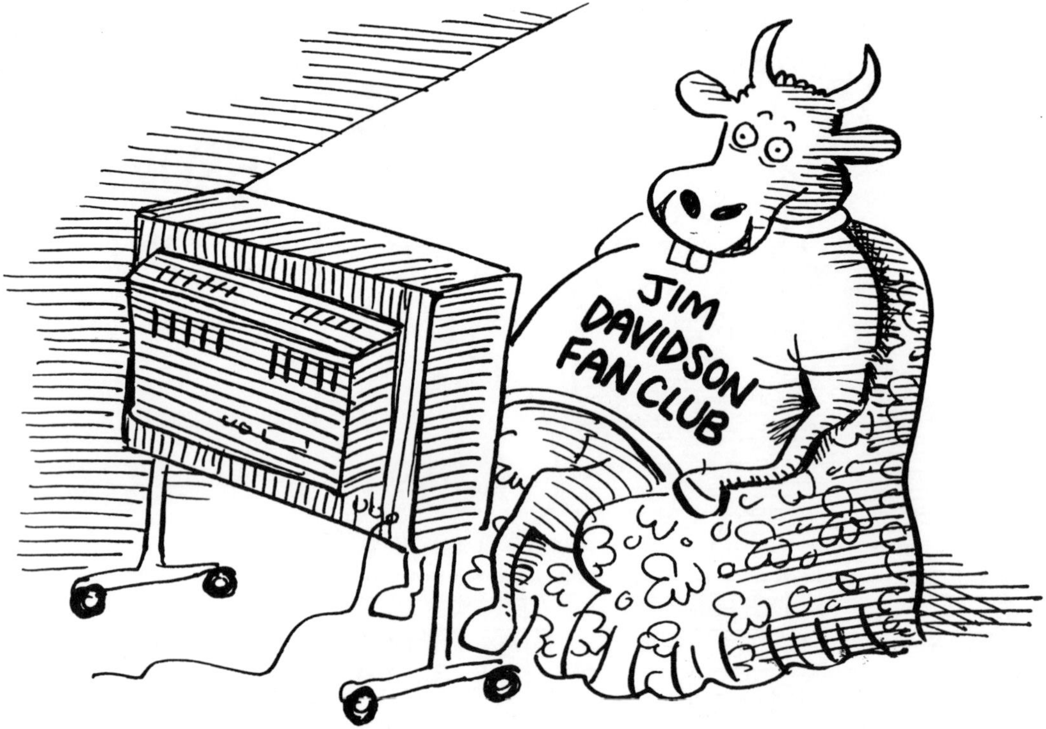
JIM
DAVIDSON
FAN CLUB

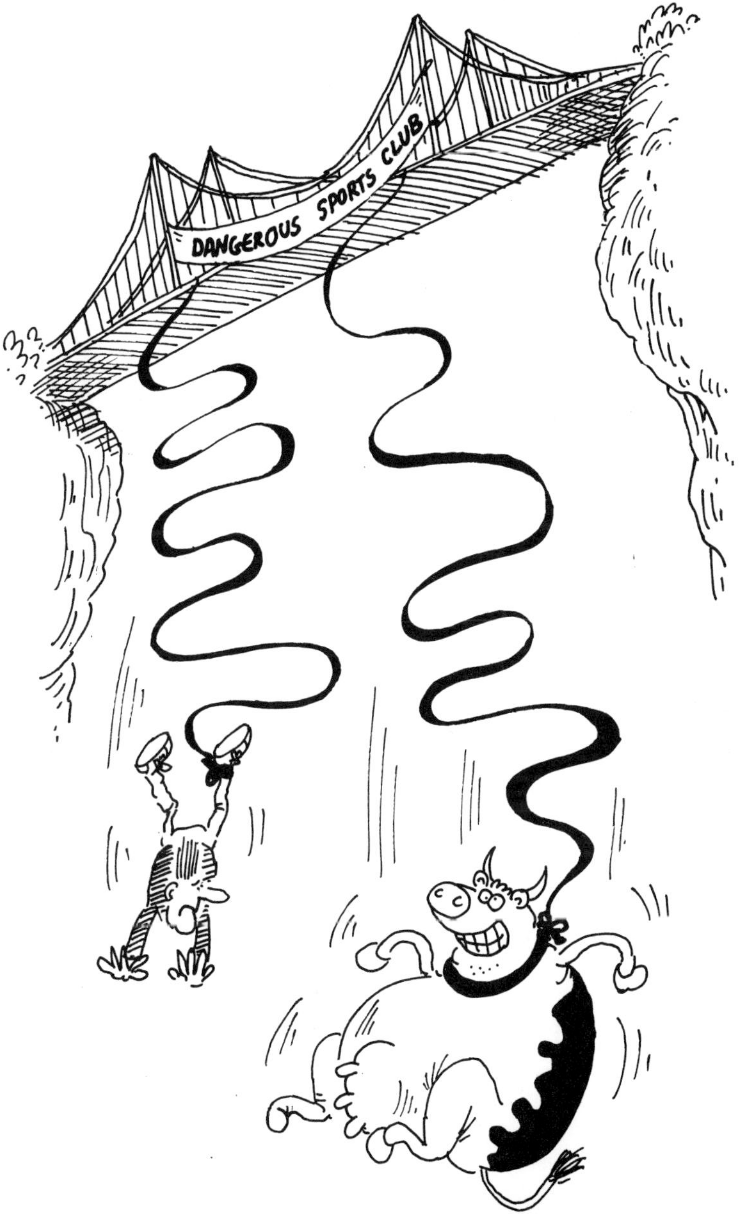
DANGEROUS SPORTS CLUB

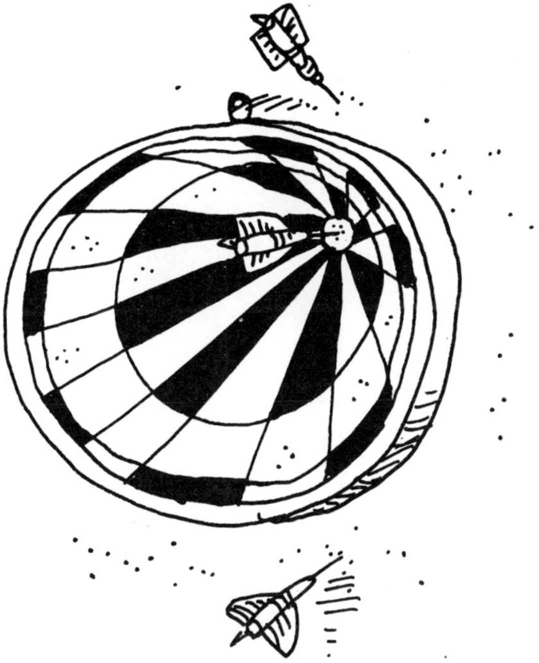

MAD BULLSEYE

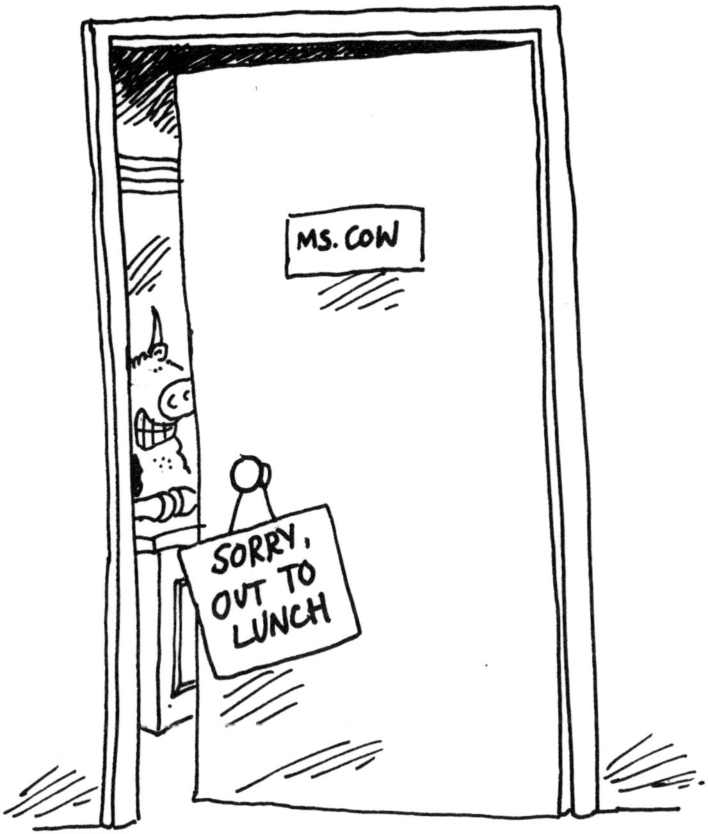
MS. COW
SORRY, OUT TO LUNCH

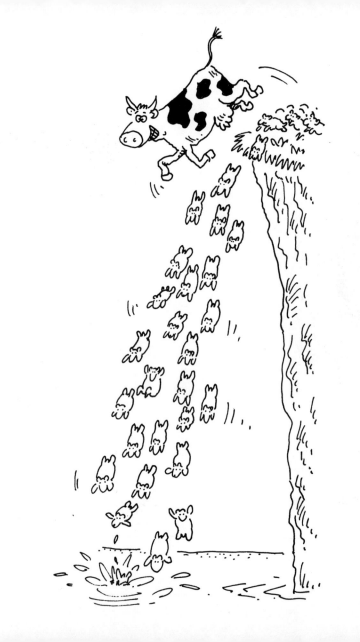

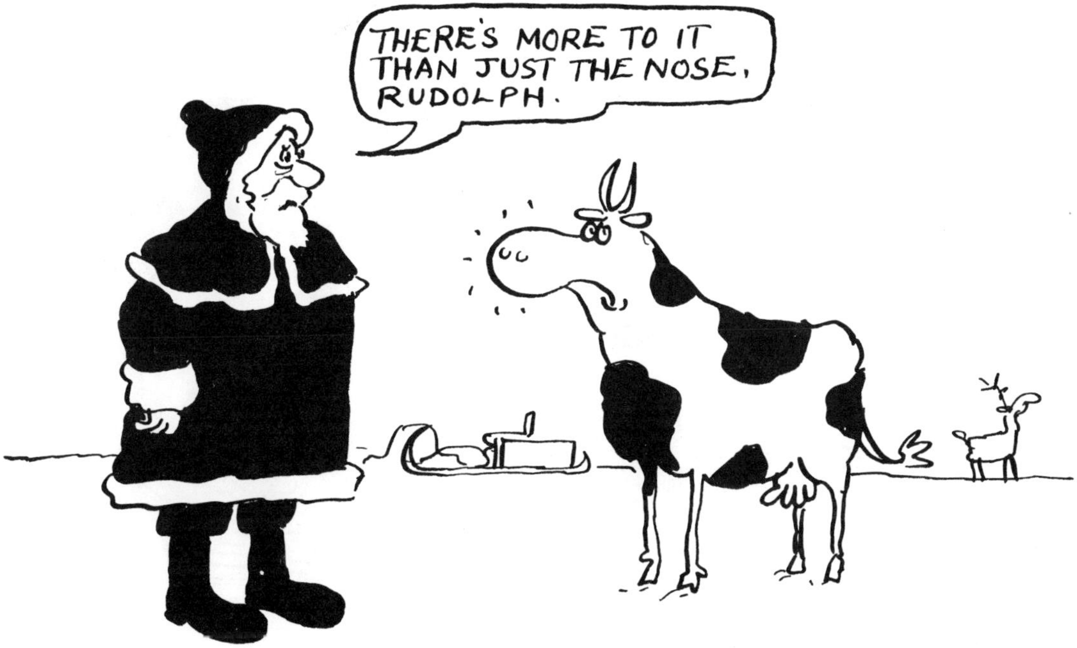
THERE'S MORE TO IT THAN JUST THE NOSE, RUDOLPH.

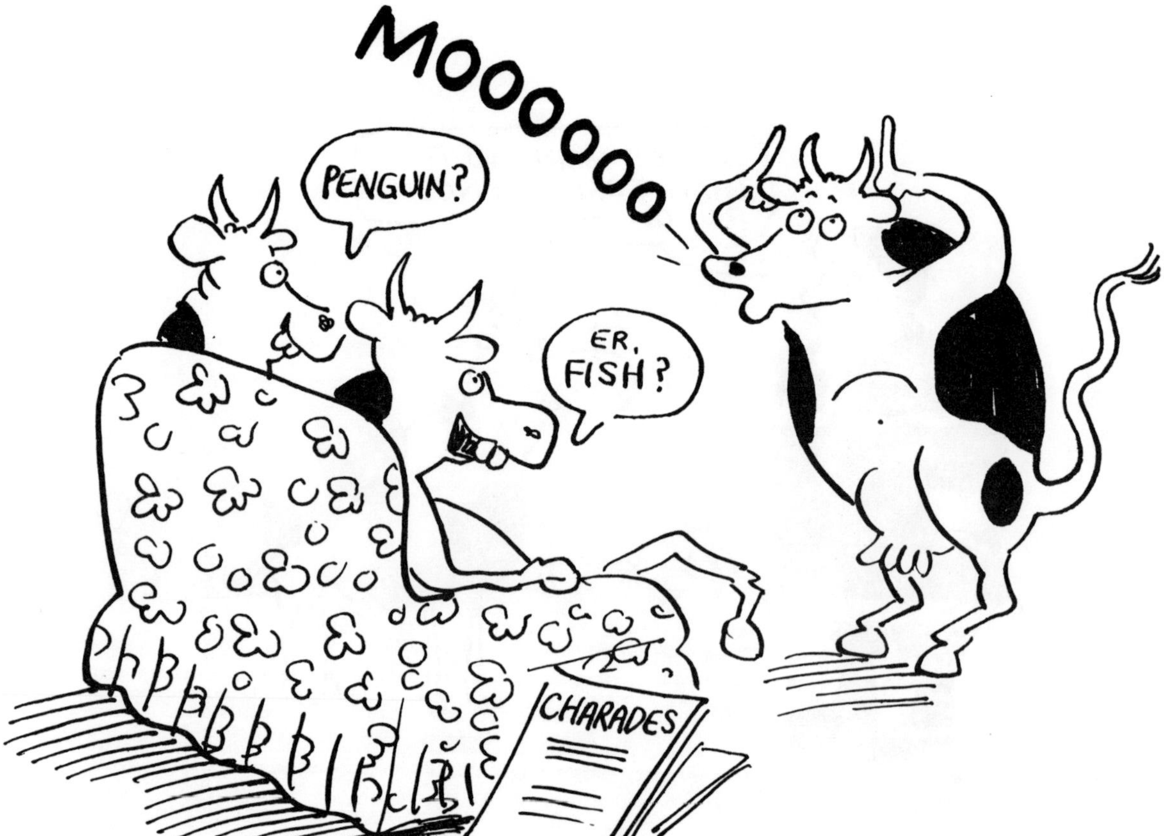
MOOOOOOO
PENGUIN?
ER, FISH?
CHARADES

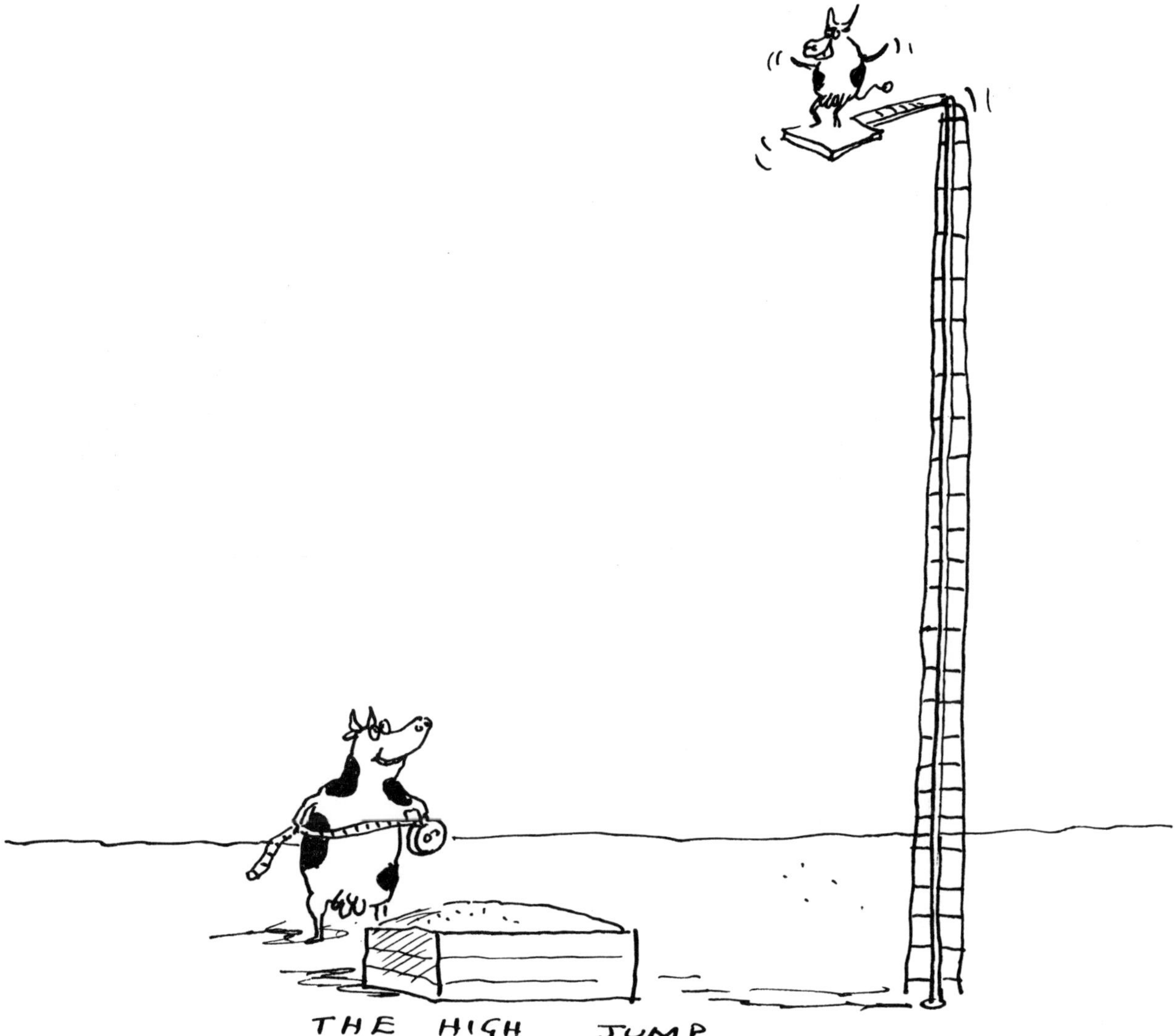

THE HIGH JUMP.

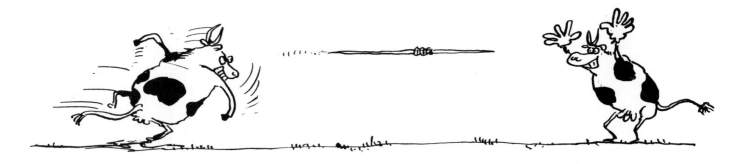

CATCHING THE JAVELIN.

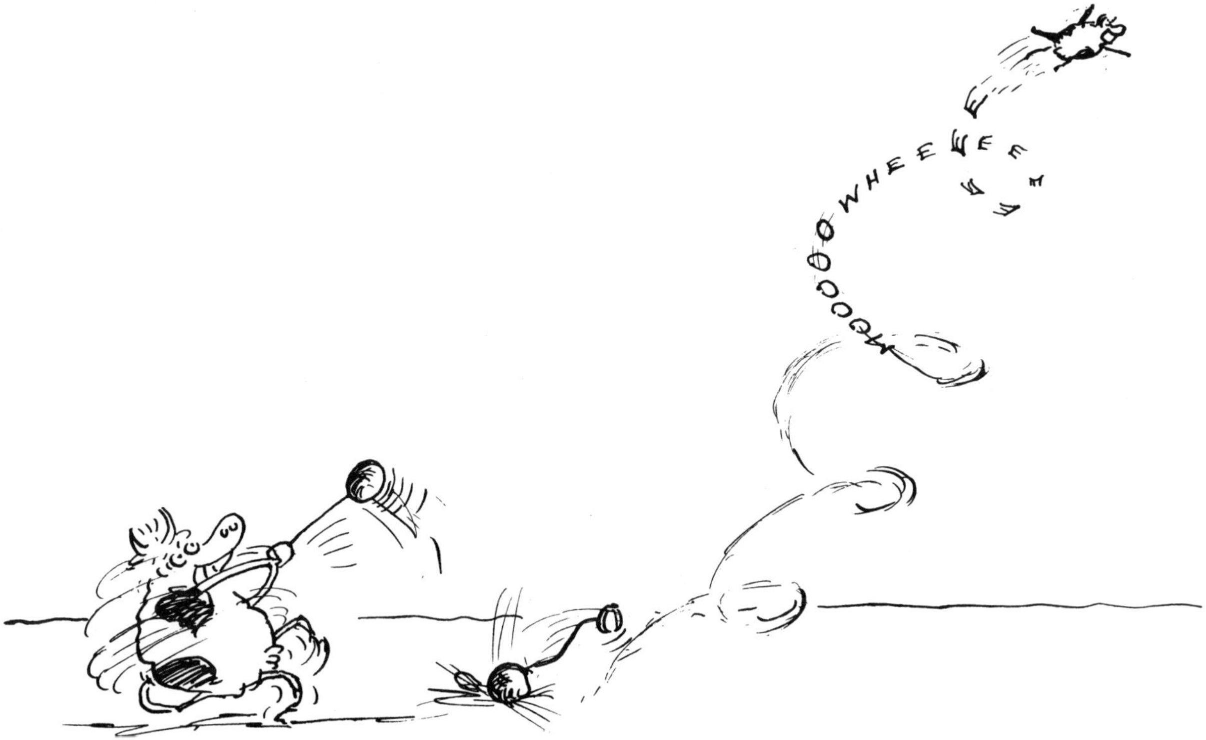
MOOOOOOOWHEEEEE

THROWING THE HAMMER.

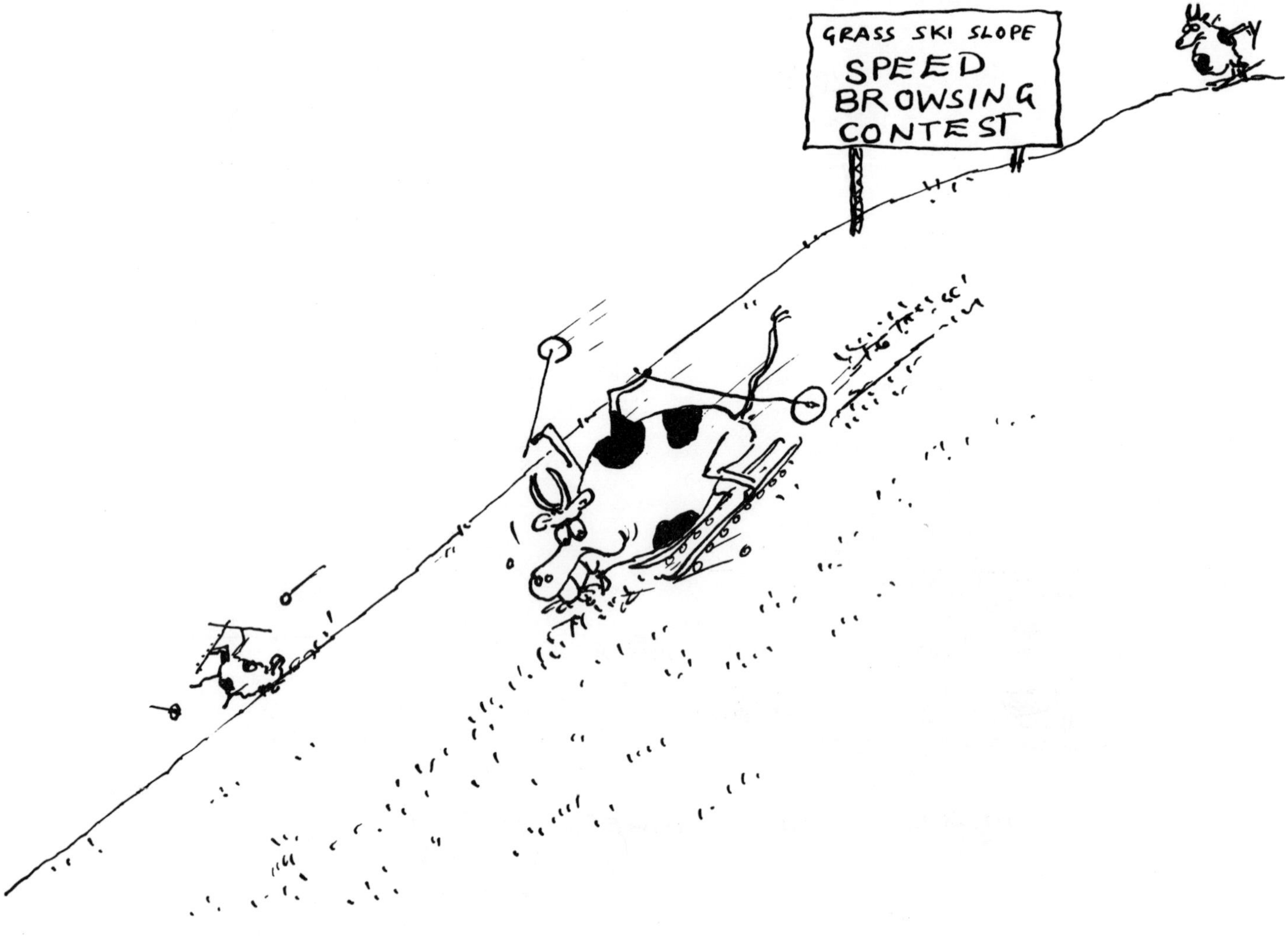
GRASS SKI SLOPE
SPEED
BROWSING
CONTEST

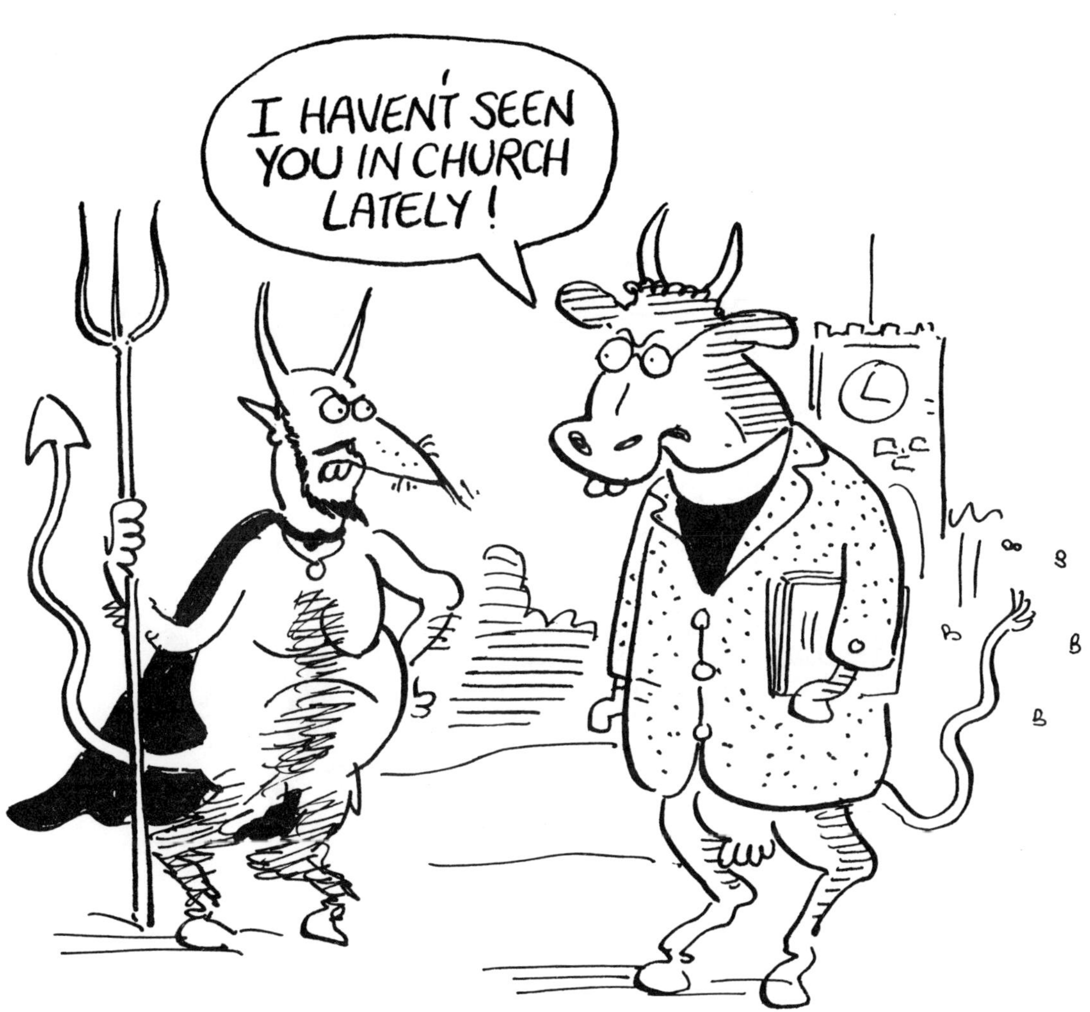
I HAVEN'T SEEN YOU IN CHURCH LATELY!

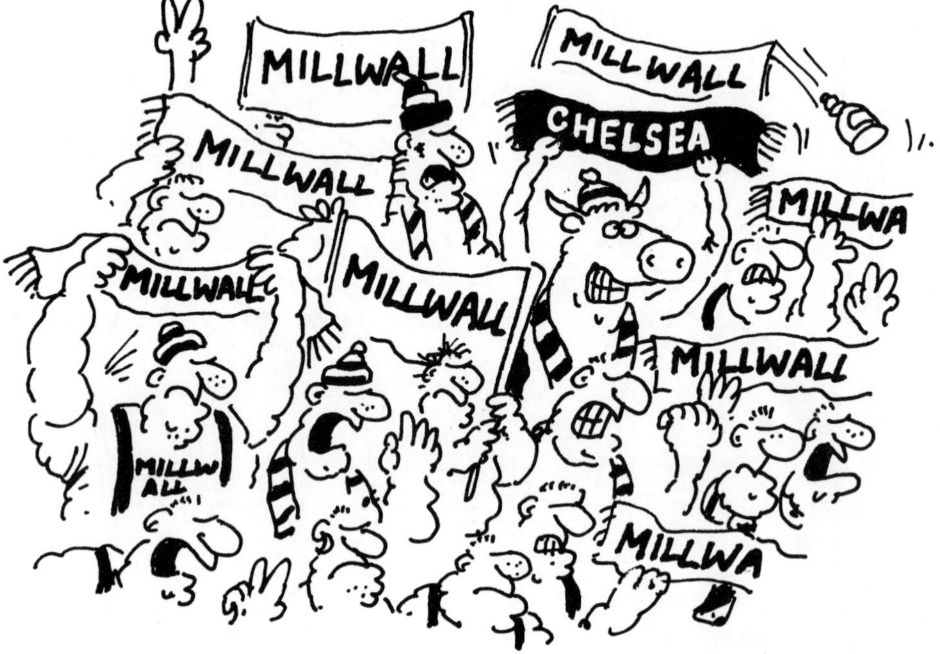
MILLWALL
MILLWALL
CHELSEA
MILLWALL
MILLWA
MILLWALL
MILLWALL
MILLWALL
MILLW ALL
MILLWA

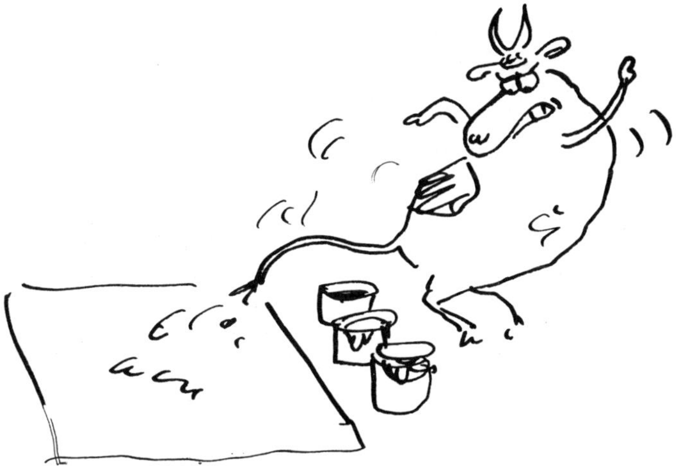

Jackson Bullock

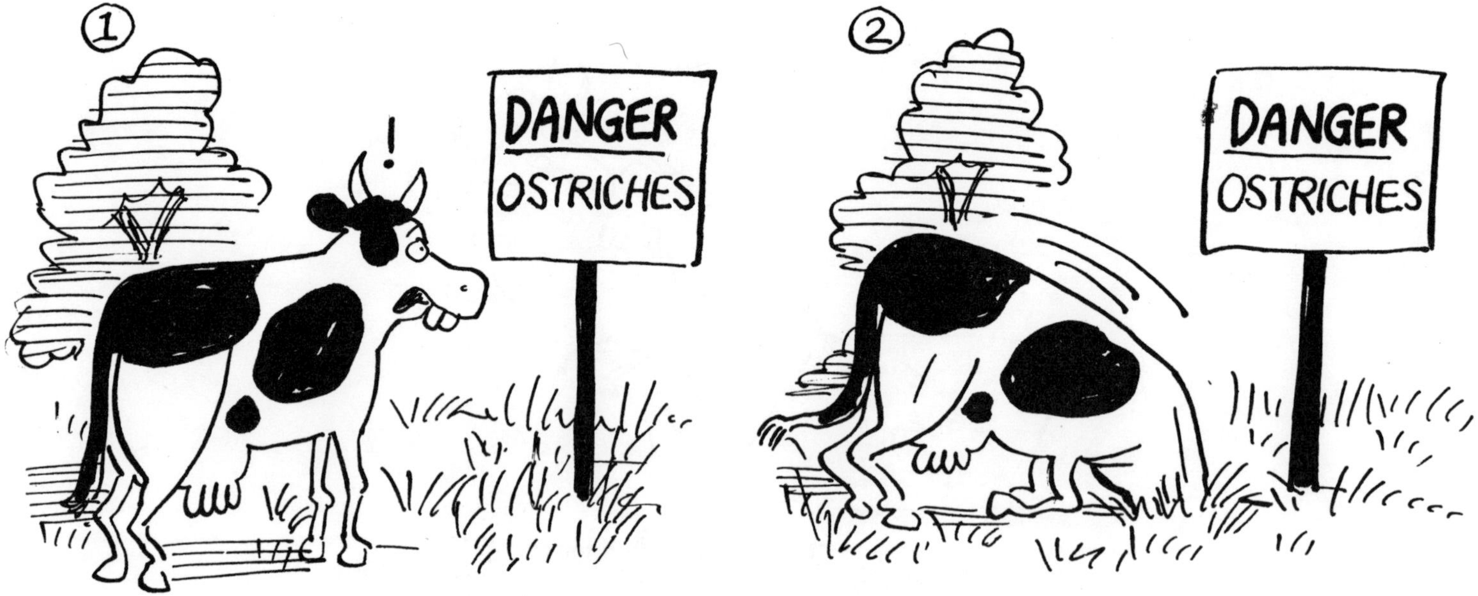
1
DANGER
OSTRICHES
2
DANGER
OSTRICHES

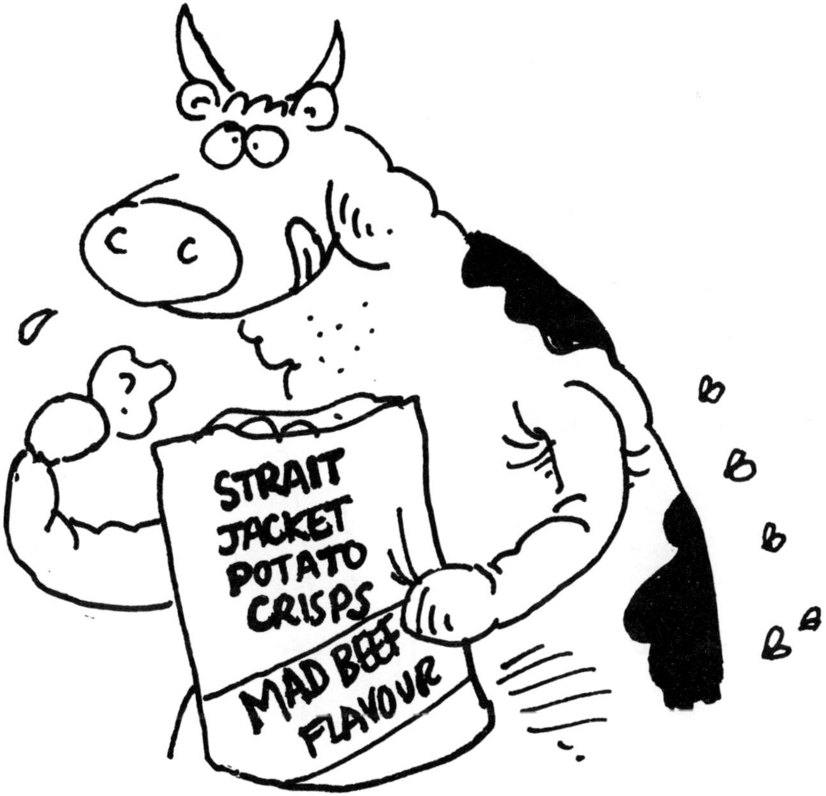
STRAIT
JACKET
POTATO
CRISPS
MAD BEEF
FLAVOUR

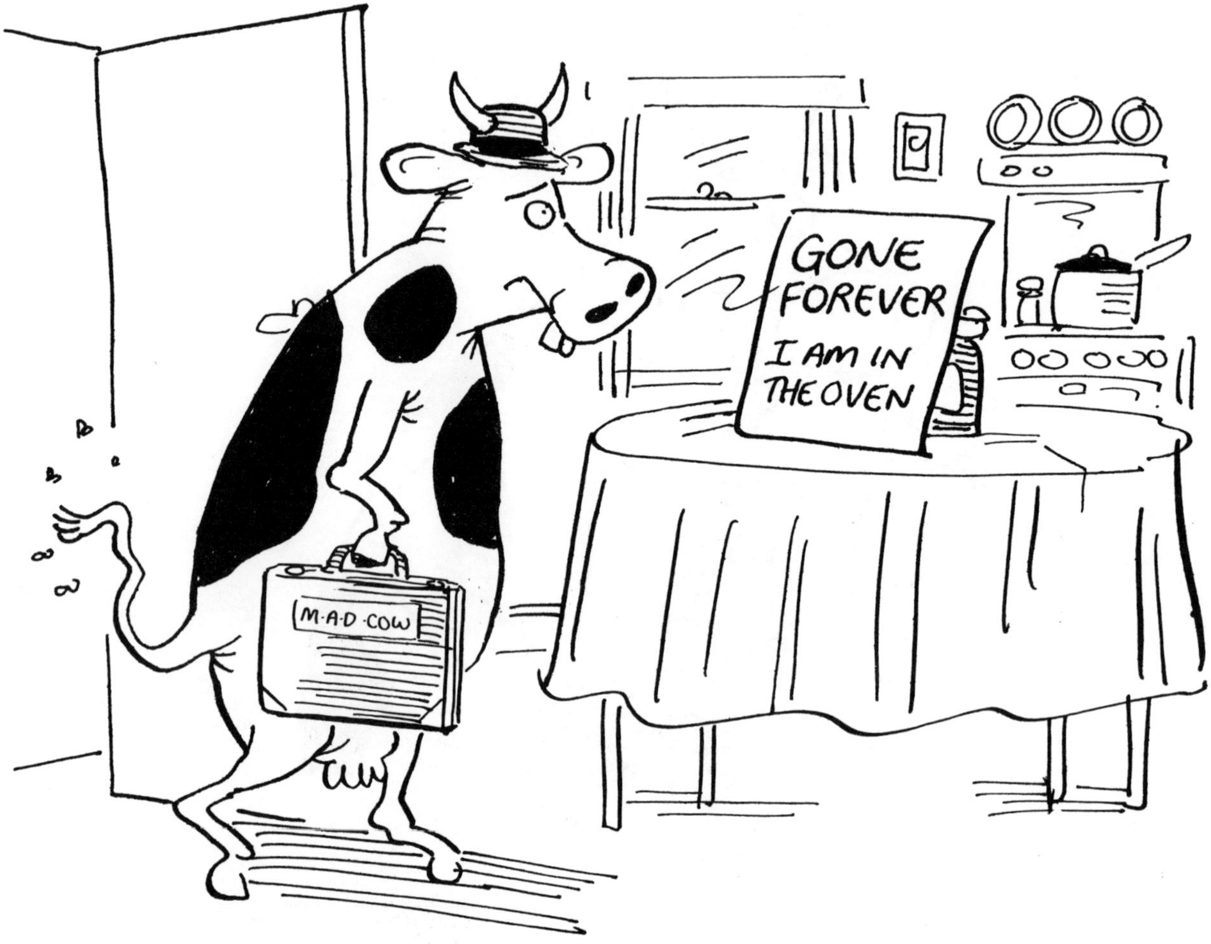
GONE FOREVER
I AM IN THE OVEN
M·A·D·COW

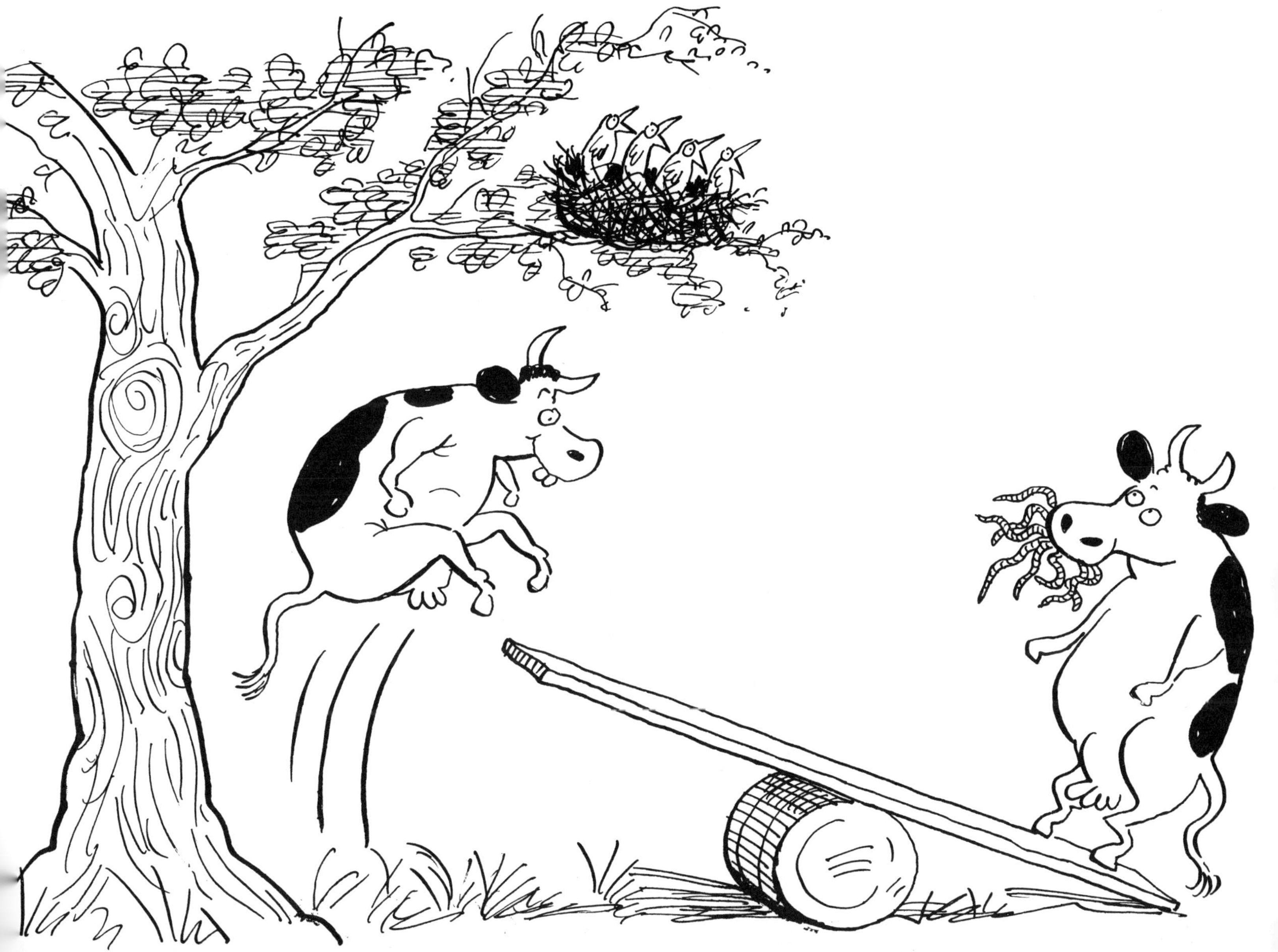

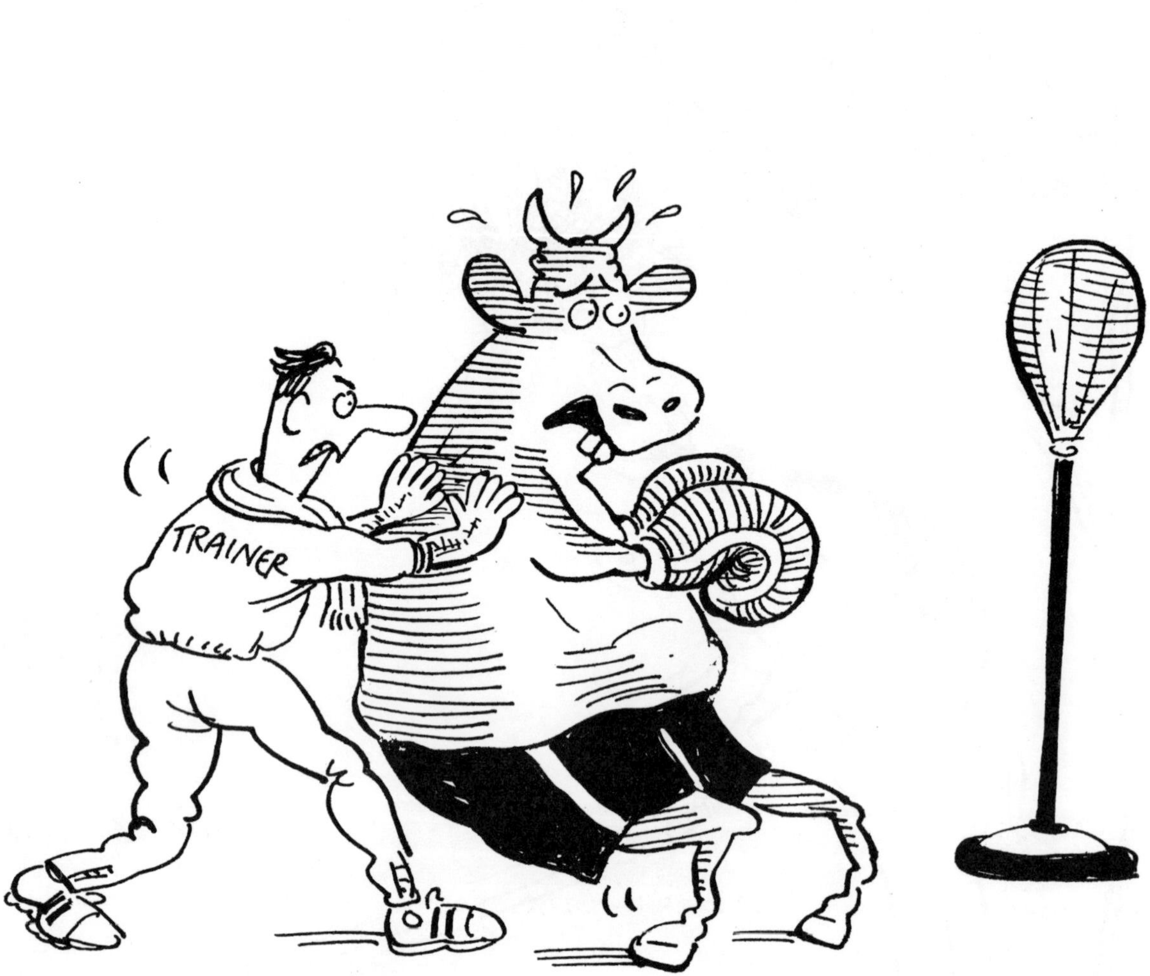
TRAINER

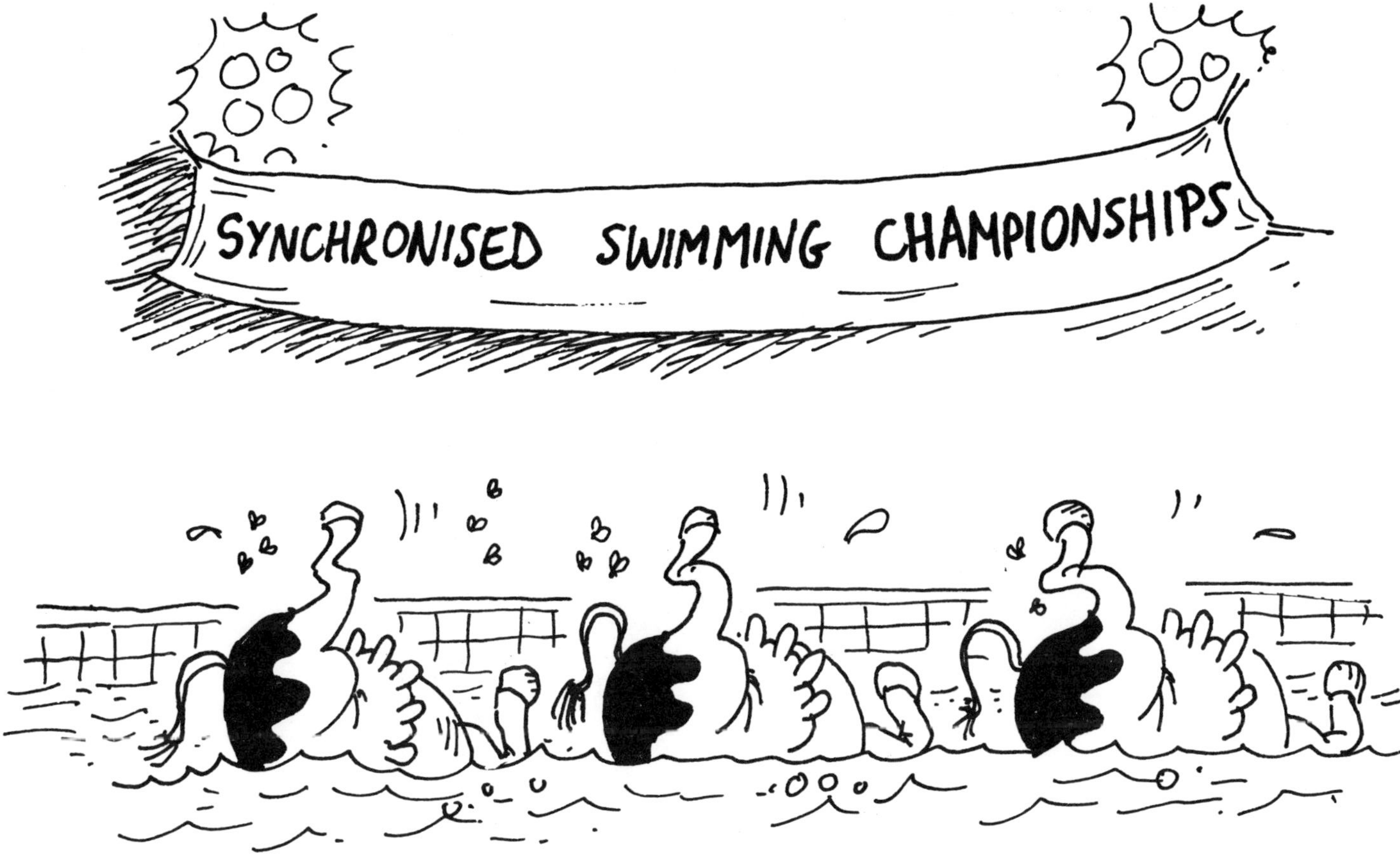
SYNCHRONISED SWIMMING CHAMPIONSHIPS

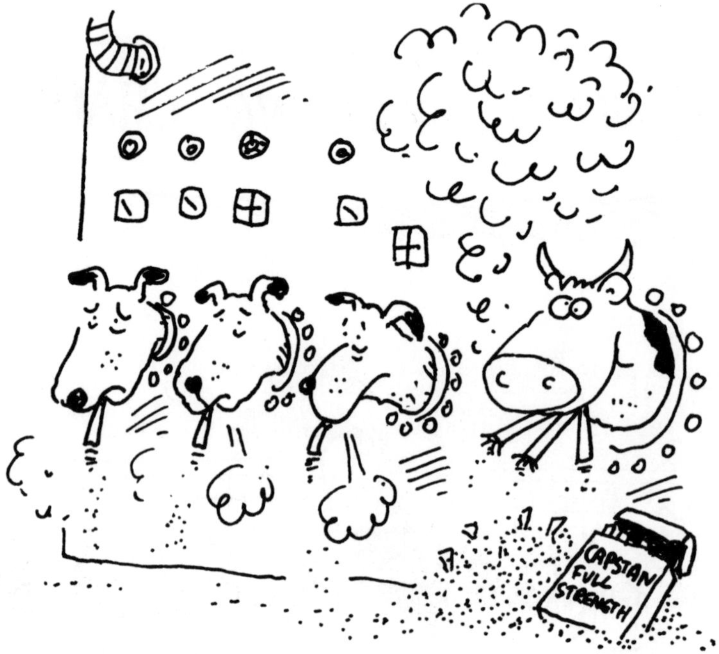
CAPSTAN
FULL
STRENGTH

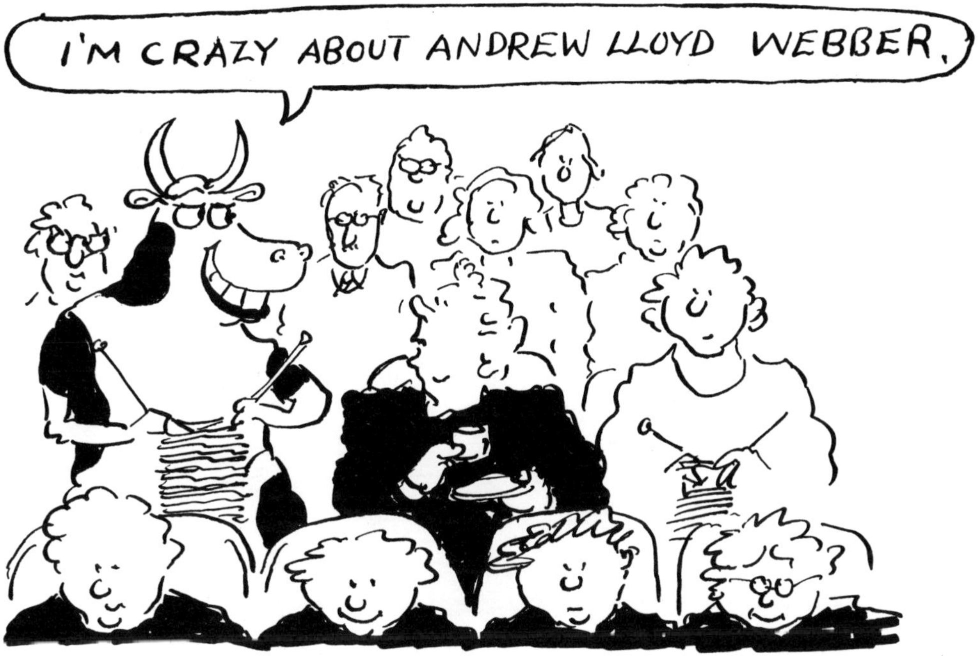
I'M CRAZY ABOUT ANDREW LLOYD WEBBER.

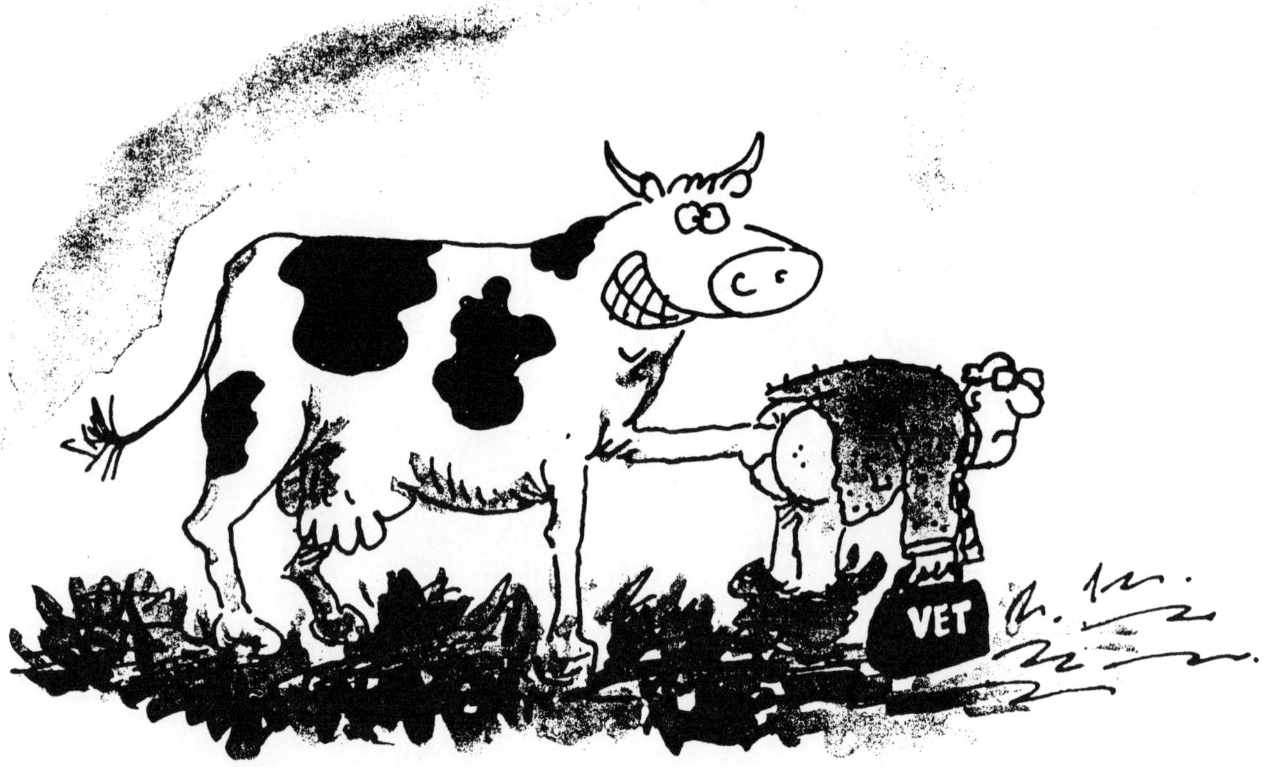
VET